10
11
9
12
15
14
13
16
8
17
18
1

99th U.S. Open

Pinehurst

Writer
Robert Sommers

Photographers
Michael Cohen
Fred Vuich

Editor
Bev Norwood

ISBN 1-878843-25-7

Statistics produced by Unisys Corporation

Course illustrations by Dan Wardlaw © The Majors of Golf

Photographs on page 7 courtesy of Tufts Archives of the Given Memorial Library (James W. Tufts) and USGA (Donald Ross and Richard S. Tufts)

Published by International Merchandising Corporation,
1360 East Ninth Street, Cleveland, Ohio 44114

Designed and produced by Davis Design

Printed in the United States of America

99th U.S. Open

Official Annual Presented by

ROLEX

In a way, this salute to Payne Stewart, who joined an exclusive group of players holding multiple victories in the U.S. Open Championship with his dramatic triumph at Pinehurst, comes a year late. In 1998, Payne let a four-stroke lead get away from him in the last round at Olympic Club and the gritty Lee Janzen instead became a double U.S. Open winner after going three years without a victory. At Pinehurst, though, Stewart refused to be denied his second Open Championship just when it looked like it might happen again.

In one of the more gripping finishes in U.S. Open history, Payne tenaciously held on and fought back on the final holes. He holed three wonderful putts, topped by the stunning 15-footer on the 18th green that gave him the one-shot victory over Phil Mickelson, who surely had to be expecting a playoff as he watched his chance for his first major disappear just as Payne's ball did when it reached the hole on the 18th green.

It was a most interesting and unique U.S. Open. Good old Pinehurst Number 2 lived up to expectations, certainly to mine at least, and justified the decision of the U.S. Golf Association to take its championship there for the first time.

This chronicle of the 1999 U.S. Open is the 15th in a series presented by Rolex Watch USA, which turns all of its proceeds over to the USGA for use in helping to fund its junior golf programs. It is my pleasure to invite you to relive the 1999 Open through the words and photographs on the pages that follow.

99th U.S. Open

Pinehurst

Set in the sandhills of central North Carolina, the Village of Pinehurst lies a short distance west of Fayetteville, close to the town of Southern Pines, where the old Seaboard Airline, a railroad nicknamed the Chicken Bone Express, clattered through the heart of town while passengers munched their fried chicken lunches.

While the two towns are within a 10-minute drive of one another, they seem unrelated. The Moore County Hunt is based in Southern Pines, while the Pinehurst Resort & Country Club and its eight golf courses set the tone for this charming replica of an old New England village. It is only fitting that it does, since its founder, James Walker Tufts, came to the region from Massachusetts. With direction by Tufts, Frederick Law Olmstead, the architect of New York City's Central Park, laid out the town.

He centered the town around the village green and routed its narrow streets so they twist and curl back on themselves as if they had been laid out by a crazed pretzel maker. Yet the idiosyncratic meanderings of its lanes and byways did not discourage those who chose to live by them.

In the past, Pinehurst had been the home of Horace Rackham, an original investor in Henry Ford's automobile company, of Eberhard Faber, who made all those pencils, and of General George C. Marshall, Army Chief of Staff during the Second World War. Later, as Secretary of State, he organized the Marshall Plan, the relief program that rebuilt post-war Europe.

After her career as a sharpshooter with Buffalo Bill's Wild West Show, Annie Oakley settled there and ran the gun club.

Prominent people in golf lived there as well. Donald Ross, the great designer of golf courses, lived by the third and fifth greens of the Number 2 Course, and Richard S. Tufts, the grandson of the founder, owned a house by the second hole.

Marshall had a small, white clapboard house not far from the Carolina Hotel. But then, nothing in Pinehurst is far from the Carolina, a gracious old building where before 1970 men wore coats at breakfast and coats and ties at dinner (before the Second World War, black tie was not uncommon).

Wander out to the Carolina's portico, pausing first to fit a piece or two into a jigsaw puzzle that is always in the lobby, and there in the distance sits the clubhouse of the Pinehurst Country Club, one of golf's treasures. Five courses branch out from the clubhouse — the Numbers 1, 2, 3, 4 and 5. Over the years three more have been added, and now Pinehurst claims eight courses, Numbers 6, 7 and 8 on ground not far from its grand old clubhouse.

Almost from the start, golf has been the heart of Pinehurst. In springtime, golfers flock to the region, eager to test themselves against a collection of courses both at Pinehurst and surrounding towns. All the visitors want at least one round over Pinehurst's Number 2 course. Known internationally simply as Number 2, it ranks among the world's best.

Because golf became so important to Pinehurst, Pinehurst became important to golf as well. With this background, there was a time not long ago when membership in the Pinehurst Country Club amounted to a status symbol. It was a matter of pride; Pinehurst's background of wonderful

The eighth hole, par 4 and 485 yards.

courses and extraordinary winners of its tournaments inspired a sense of being part of something special. No wonder a man from New Jersey snapped up the offer of a membership by saying, "Hell yes, I'll join. It's worth the fee to add Pinehurst to my obituary."

Not that Pinehurst charged exorbitant fees; a check for $20 covered the dues, and memberships were passed out like receipts for green fees. That didn't matter; the name alone carried such prestige, members felt they had climbed Olympus.

First of all, all the great golfers had played Number 2 in the series of North and South tournaments — the Open, Amateur and Women's Amateur. Before the resort fell out of the hands of the Tufts family, the Professional Golfers' Association of America had taken the 1936 PGA Championship and the 1951 Ryder Cup to Number 2 as well, and the USGA had taken the 1962 United States Amateur there.

Francis Ouimet and Chick Evans had won there, and Walter Travis had won the North and South Amateur in its early years; George Dunlap, a marvelous golfer in his time, won six North and South Amateurs from 1931 through 1942; Harvie Ward and Frank Stranahan played two gripping final matches in 1948 and 1949 (Ward won the first by one hole, and Stranahan won the second by 2 and 1). In one unforgettable series, Hillman Robbins, Bill Campbell, Dick Chapman and Jack Nicklaus won consecutive championships. Chapman, who had a house in Pinehurst, had won the 1940 National Amateur, and the other three would win it within a short time.

Number 2 had been a proving ground for Billy Joe Patton, a lively North Carolinian whose backswing was a blur but who could escape any jail it put him in. Shortly after Patton nearly won the 1954 Masters, he won the North and South Amateur. Forever linked to Pinehurst, Patton won twice more in the early 1960s.

Curtis Strange won twice in succession; Corey Pavin won, along with Hal Sutton and Davis Love III.

The great women golfers made their statements at Pinehurst as well. Glenna Collett Vare won six North and South championships, Barbara McIntire won five, Maureen Orcutt won three in succession, Louise Suggs won three, Marlene Streit won twice, and the great Estelle Lawson Page won seven women's championships over 11 seasons.

Ben Hogan began his reign among the game's pre-eminent players by winning the 1940 North and South Open, the first tournament he'd won after eight years of trying. Over the next 10 days he won two more, at Greensboro and Asheville, N.C. — three tournaments in 13 days. Walter Hagen won three North and South Opens, along with Sam Snead and Hogan. In successive years it was won by Horton Smith, who had won two Masters Tournaments, Vic Ghezzi, a PGA champion, then Byron Nelson, Hogan, Snead and Hogan again. Cary Middlecoff won in 1945 as an amateur.

In June 1999 this singular course took on more luster as the site of the 99th United States Open Championship, golf's most important competition, only the second Open played south of the Potomac and east of the Mississippi (the 1976 championship went to Atlanta).

Even though the 1999 championship was Pinehurst's first U.S. Open, the course deserved the chance. It is an absolute jewel. Ross worked on it nearly 50 years. From the time he came to Pinehurst until he died, in 1948, he tinkered with it endlessly.

Strangely enough, golf had no part in Tufts' original concept for his resort. He had begun his career as a clerk in an apothecary shop, later opened his own store, and eventually put together a string of small shops around Boston. Most apothecaries, or drug stores, featured soda fountains. A shrewd man, Tufts improved on the current soda fountain and eventually became president of the American Soda Fountain Company.

A wealthy man by the late 19th century, he experienced respiratory illnesses much of his life and felt he might improve his health by escaping the cold New England winters. He pictured building a resort for those not wealthy enough to winter in

James W. Tufts

Donald Ross

Richard S. Tufts

Florida, and so he chose the sandhills of North Carolina, partway between the New England snows and Florida's sunshine, where the winter air remained dry and mild and the soft breezes carried the crisp scent of pine.

Tufts found a 5,000-acre patch called The Barrens, a parcel of over-harvested forest near Southern Pines, and bought it in 1895 for $1 an acre. Hearing the news, those who knew the land said Tufts made a bad deal.

Unmoved, Tufts built a village green, a church and a post office, the first steps toward creating his little town.

During its first two seasons, Pinehurst offered its guests the normal fare of a proper spa — croquet, carriage rides, bird walks and card games. Then some guests brought golf clubs along and began peppering grazing cattle with flying balls. Responding to the demand, Tufts himself laid out a rough nine holes. A year later he built another nine holes, and in 1900 Harry Vardon and J.H. Taylor played there during their first visit to the United States, the tour climaxed by Vardon's winning the U.S. Open and Taylor's finishing second.

At about this time Robert Wilson, a Harvard professor who had become smitten by the game in Scotland, lured Donald Ross to the United States to become the professional at the Oakley Golf Club, in Massachusetts.

Ross was a versatile man. He had apprenticed as a club maker in St. Andrews under Robert Forgan, one of the more successful foundries of the 19th century, came under the spell of Old Tom Morris for a time, and then worked under John Sutherland, the celebrated secretary at Royal Dornoch, which Morris had helped design. Ross was 13 in 1886 when he watched Morris and Sutherland build Dornoch's first nine holes. Sutherland himself did the second nine.

After his time in St. Andrews, Ross moved back to Dornoch, where he had been born, and spent seven years as professional and greenkeeper at the Dornoch Golf Club. Those seven years, and the few at St. Andrews, affected young Ross profoundly. At nightfall, he and Sutherland would walk the course together, studying how it might be improved and discussing the basis of good golf course architecture. Those walks and some tutoring by Old Tom turned Ross into one of the greatest designers of golf courses.

Eventually Ross settled in the United States. He arrived in Boston in 1899, took the job at Oakley, and became friendly with the Tufts family. James Tufts had been looking for a winter professional and offered Ross the job, beginning an association with Pinehurst that lasted through Ross' lifetime.

Besides serving as Pinehurst's winter professional (he worked at Oakley during the summer), Ross laid out Pinehurst's Numbers 1, 2 and 3 courses. They were superb for their time. As word of his architectural flair spread, offers from other clubs poured in at such a rate that by 1910 he had given up his Oakley job, expanded his design interests and moved permanently to Pinehurst. Over his career he is said to have designed about 600 courses, most of them without ever seeing the ground. A club representative would bring him a topographic map and Ross would lay out a course on paper.

The system didn't always work. Ross laid out a course in the Canadian Rockies for the Canadian Pacific railroad, whose engineers misinterpreted his intentions. He had calibrated elevations in inches, but the engineers mistook the figures for feet. A three-inch rise on the left of this green became a three-foot-high hillock and a 20-inch depression in front of another became a 20-foot-deep chasm. Unplayable when it was finished, the course was abandoned.

While Ross took no part in constructing the Canadian horror, some of those he actually worked on at the site rank among the country's very best — Oakland Hills, near Detroit; Oak Hill in Rochester, N.Y.; Inverness, in Toledo, Ohio; East Lake, in Atlanta, where Bobby Jones learned to play; Scioto, in Columbus, Ohio, where Jack Nicklaus learned to play, and the impeccable Seminole, in North Palm Beach, Fla.

Ross' most lasting treasure, though, remains the great Number 2 course at Pinehurst. Laid out first in 1903, it was rebuilt in 1935 and made into the course we have come to know.

By some accounts, Bobby Jones had wanted Ross to design the new course he planned in Augusta, Ga. Ross seemed the logical choice since Jones had grown up playing at East Lake, but when Jones lost in the first round of the 1929 U.S. Amateur, at Pebble Beach, he stayed long enough to play Cypress Point. He fell in love with it, and gave the Augusta job to Alister Mackenzie, Cypress Point's designer. Disappointed, Ross turned his energies to Number 2.

In their original form, all the Pinehurst courses had sand greens, but with the PGA Championship coming in 1936, the changeover to grass had to be made. In March 1935, Paul Runyan shot 276 and became the last man to win the North and South Open on sand greens. By the next spring, Number 2's greens had been converted to grass.

Sand greens were simply flat, mostly circular spots with no contour and no shaping. They were strange to play as well. If the ground was soft and wet, a ball would simply go splat and stay where it hit; if the ground was dry, the ball might take a high bounce and run away.

Taking advantage of the decision to switch from sand, Rose completely rebuilt Number 2. First he lengthened it and used the sandy rough to shape and turn the fairways. Then he worked magic on the greens, which have become a landmark in golf. He dug up every one of them, and using horse-drawn drag-pans, he sculpted the ground around them and used the soil to crest the putting surfaces and shape the mounds and hillocks that still influence how the ball behaves. He made the greens big, but at the same time left only parts of them suitable for hole placement.

While the greens average about 6,000 square feet, which seems comfortable, their effective size is about half that. Every one resembles the turtle's back; they slope away at the sides and backs and ask for particular emphasis on the short game.

Ross created greens the golf course architect Rees Jones believes are unique.

"Some courses have one or two crowned

The second hole, par 4 and 447 yards.

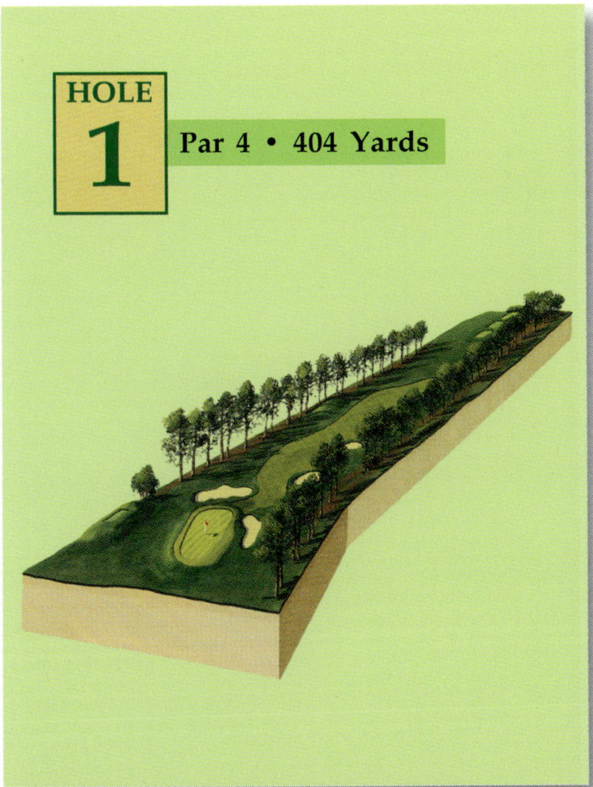

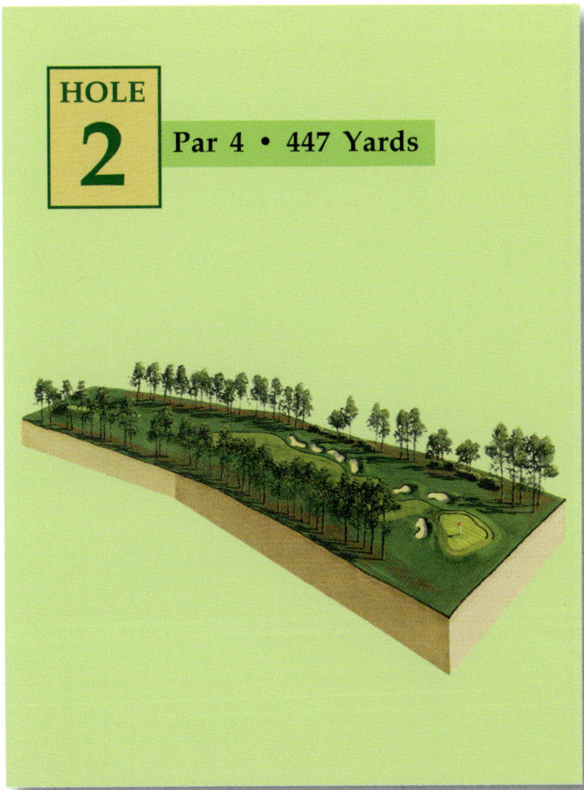

greens, but not all 18," he claimed. "There's not another course like this."

Those close to the game think of Number 2 as the game's prime examination of the short game; a missed green insists on deft chipping and pitching to save par. The greens' unusual design sets up plenty of opportunity to play the little pitches and chips that can make or break a round. Approach shots that appear reasonably well played often catch a downslope and scoot into a hollow or a bunker, behind a knoll, or occasionally drift into the rough.

If the 1999 Open proved anything, it demonstrated that chipping at Number 2 is seldom easy. Per-Ulrik Johansson, a regular on the PGA European Tour, missed the eighth green, chipped twice with a 3-wood, the newest fad among tour players, and watched the ball roll back to his feet. His third attempt, with a putter, stayed on, and he made 7. After his short pitch rolled off the side of the fifth green, Jesper Parnevik pitched from one side of the green over the other, which left him so timid he left his next shot yards short of the hole, then applauded himself when he holed out to save a double bogey. Opening the third round, Tiger Woods chipped all the way over the first green and double-bogeyed. Plenty of others failed the test.

In the last round John Daly missed the eighth green and didn't play his run-up chip firmly enough. When the ball began rolling back toward him, he rapped it while it was still in motion, violating not only the rules of the game but its etiquette as well. Counting a two-stroke penalty for hitting a moving ball, Daly scored 11 at a par 4 and closed with 83.

No one knows if Ross designed his greens to behave so mischievously as they did in the Open, but he was a strong-willed man. He held the job as Pinehurst manager at a time when the caddies declared a strike. Angered, Ross carried a 5-iron into the caddie yard and asked for the ringleader. When one of the bigger and older caddies stepped forward, Ross tapped the club on the man's shoulder and hissed, "If you don't

The sixth hole, par 3 and 222 yards.

Hole 5 — **Par 4 • 482 Yards**

Hole 6 — **Par 3 • 222 Yards**

get back to work, I'll bounce this 5-iron off your head." The strike had ended.

In what little spare time he had, Ross grew roses. Peter V. Tufts, the great-grandson of Pinehurst's founder, remembers his garden on a spare lot next to his house.

"I'm not talking about a rose bush here and there," Tufts said. "He grew top-notch, showcase roses."

In designing his courses, particularly Number 2, Ross believed in creating a natural look. When the entire course was covered by common bermudagrass, someone standing on the first tee might not be able to make out the first green. Both the tee, nothing more than a level place on the ground, and the green blended perfectly into the contours of the ground.

He believed in natural looking rough as well, not the wild and tangled grass so common at many courses. Instead, he bordered the cultivated fairways with sandy wastes spotted with the tough, clumpy wire grass that grows naturally in the sandhills.

We'll never know if Ross was totally satisfied with Number 2 when he died, but the Tufts family — James' son Leonard and Leonard's son Richard — maintained Number 2 as Ross had left it.

It changed in 1970 when the resort passed from the Tufts to the Diamondhead Corporation. This was a bitter moment in the Pinehurst legacy. Richard S. Tufts had become a powerful figure in golf. An outright authority on the rules of the game, he had progressed through the chairs of the United States Golf Association as chairman of the Association's three most important committees — Implements and Ball, Championship and Rules of Golf. After this apprenticeship, he was elected president in 1956 and 1957. Richard Tufts also wrote and published two books — *The Principles Behind The Rules of Golf* and *The Scottish Invasion. Principles* became a classic; *Scottish Invasion* didn't. When Richard asked his son, Peter, how many he should have printed, Peter suggested 10,000. It sold maybe 300.

Richard was devoted to Pinehurst, but

The seventh hole, par 4 and 398 yards.

The 13th hole, par 4 and 383 yards.

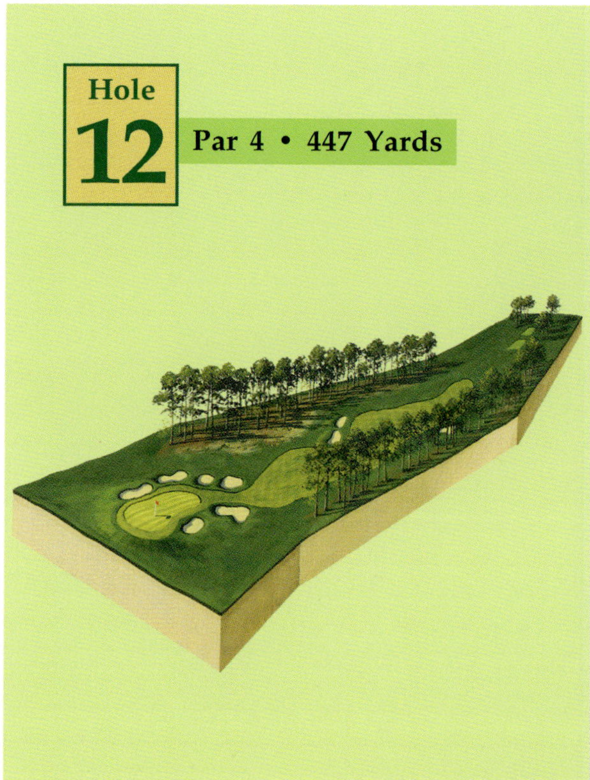

his two brothers, James and Albert, along with Bill Sledge, who owned about 20 percent of the company, wanted to sell. Since they controlled more than 60 percent of the stock, Richard had no choice. It was sold, and it changed immediately.

Believing it was upgrading Number 2, Diamondhead scraped the sandy wastes clear of wire grass, sprigged bermudagrass from tree-line to tree-line and planted the greens in bentgrass. Diamondhead also staged a few PGA Tour tournaments. After struggling with Number 2 for three years, posting winning scores of 281, 280 and 274, the professionals ripped it apart in 1977. Hale Irwin shot 65-62-69-68–264, Leonard Thompson was next with 269, and 17 others shot under 280. The grand old course had lost its sting.

After a few years Diamondhead neglected Pinehurst and eventually sold it to Club Corporation of America, which operates a number of golf properties. Evidently with a better feel for the game, Club Corp. set about restoring Number 2 to what it had been. Then, about six years before the 1999 Open, the company brought in Rees Jones for a massive overhaul.

The youngest son of Robert Trent Jones, Rees had visited Pinehurst some years earlier. Working for his father in Montclair, N.J., but living in New York City, Rees had been dating Susan Singleton. When she invited him to a wedding, Rees didn't want to go. When she told him the wedding was in Pinehurst, he rushed home to pack his bag, and he and Susan drove all night. He was on the first tee of Number 2 at 8 o'clock the next morning. Susan went to bed.

That was a Saturday. Sunday night he proposed and she accepted. He had become even more fond of Pinehurst.

When Irwin shot his 264 in 1977, Number 2 played to 7,007 yards. Rees found tees where nobody had ever thought to look and stretched it out to 7,300 yards. The USGA, in its compassion, decided not to play all of the course and cut it back to 7,175 yards, only microscopically more manageable.

After taking exquisite measurements

The 15th hole, par 3 and 202 yards.

using exotic electronic gadgets, Jones followed Ross' steps from 1935. He dug up every green and rebuilt their bases to USGA specifications and planted them to a new strain of bentgrass that survives in hot and humid weather.

He dug out every bunker as well and found about three feet of sand in them. Explaining why he had dug out the bunkers, Jones said he found that over the years the grounds staff had simply dumped sand in them every year, and over time they had become more shallow than the original plan.

"We lowered every bunker by almost three feet," he said.

Meantime, the sandy wastes were restored along the fairways' flanks and replanted with native wire grass. Now Number 2 looked as it was supposed to look.

The players loved it. Lee Janzen, who had won the 1998 championship at Olympic, in San Francisco, said Number 2 showed that architects "can create hazards without digging big holes, island greens or water hazards. They do that by building difficult greens where you have to be precise with your iron play."

Stuart Appleby said, "There'll be a lot of talking to the golf ball this week. A lot of good shots will wind up 20 yards away. You're not going to be on the greens two-putting all day; you'll have to scramble and scramble."

Payne Stewart, runner-up in 1998, said that during a practice round when he was trying to determine how to chip, he tried nine different clubs.

"You'll see everyone's imagination tested," he said. "That's what's so great about Pinehurst. That's exactly what should be tested at an Open. I can't tell you the last Open played without rough around the greens, but the way this course was designed, you don't need it."

Justin Leonard said what he had to say briefly: "The golf course is U.S. Open caliber."

Stewart had a further word: "It's a gem. It's beautiful. It's phenomenal."

Titleist

99th U.S. Open

Prologue

Like old heroes, old eras die hard. Yet, the time must come when one generation loses its luster and yields to younger men. It's the natural order; it's happened to all the great players when they grew old. It happened to Hagen and Sarazen, to Hogan, Nelson and Snead, to Palmer, Trevino and Watson, and now, evidently, even to Nicklaus. The world moves on.

As the 1999 Open approached, a group of five younger players, all of them in their 20s, appeared ready to assume command of championship golf. Waving their banners highest were David Duval and Tiger Woods, with Ernie Els, Phil Mickelson and Justin Leonard close behind.

Duval and Woods had battled for the top rung in the world rankings ladder for two years. Woods held it first, then Duval passed him when his game strengthened and he learned to win. Els, of course, had already won two U.S. Opens when he checked in at Pinehurst, and Mickelson, 29, had won 13 tournaments, 12 of them after joining the PGA Tour in 1992. One year earlier, in January 1991, he had won at Tucson as an amateur.

As Duval grew into such a dominating figure over the previous two years, he had drawn attention away from Woods. Duval had simply played so much better than anyone else, he was almost unbeatable. In the previous two and a half years he had won 11 tournaments — three in 1997, including the Tour Championship, four more in 1998 and another four halfway through March of the 1999 season.

He had everything. He birdied more holes than anybody, hit more greens, ranked second in putting, drove long enough and stood at the top in scoring by averaging 69.01 strokes per round. He was the complete golfer.

David Duval had become the world's top-ranked golfer with four victories in 1999.

Where Duval had won four tournaments by June, Woods had won three, including the Deutsche Bank–SAP Open TPC of Europe two weeks before winning the Memorial Tournament. No one else had made much of a statement. Jose Maria Olazabal had won the Masters, but he had missed the 36-hole cut in three of his eight tournaments on the European circuit and one of his six in the United States. So far, then, the year belonged to Duval.

A magnetic figure since his days playing junior golf, Woods had backed off since his first, stunning, full season. Just 20 years old when he joined the Tour in August 1996, he startled golf by winning two tournaments that year and five more in 1997, including one in Thailand. The memory of his astonishing performance in the Masters will never fade. Shooting 270 at Augusta National, he broke the 32-year-old record of Jack Nicklaus and won by 12 strokes, an absurd margin. Added to that special moment, he won three other PGA Tour events as well. The following year he won only once in the United States and once in Thailand, but fighting back, he won again at San Diego early in 1999, and the Memorial just two weeks before the Open began.

Woods and Duval seemed evenly matched. Where Duval had won 11 tournaments, Woods had won nine. Both of them were capable of any kind of scoring. Duval, of course, shot that astounding 59 in the closing round of the Bob Hope Chrysler Classic in Palm Springs. In 12 events lead-

Ernie Els was seeking to win a third Open.

ing up to the Open, Duval had played 20 rounds in the 60s, some of the better scores a 63, a 64, a 65 and three 66s. On the Friday the week before the Open, however, Duval burned his right thumb and forefinger on a tea kettle, reducing his practice time to only two days.

Woods, of course, was capable of shooting anything at all. Already he had shot three 67s, two 66s, two 65s, a 62 and a 61. Blessed with the potential to erupt at any time, Woods could frighten the field. After a dismal first round of 74 at Congressional in the 1997 Open, he made everyone nervous with 67 in the second.

Somehow, though, Woods had lost his staying power, he followed his 67 with 73 and 72, much too high to challenge. Still, Woods continued to shoot outrageous scores, like his 64 at Royal Troon in the third round of the 1997 British Open and his 66 in the last round at Royal Birkdale in 1998. Sparkling as they were, they followed

Opposite, Tiger Woods entered the Open having won in his last two starts.

Phil Mickelson sought his first major title.

Justin Leonard had demonstrated his ability by winning the 1997 British Open.

loose rounds that had left him too far behind. Woods followed his 64 at Troon with 74 the next day, but while his 66 at Birkdale set the target score at 281 for Mark O'Meara and Brian Watts to shoot, he had played the previous two rounds in 73 and 77.

While Duval edged past him in the 1999 rankings, Woods still had something Duval coveted; in the Masters, Woods had won a tournament of international consequence. Duval, on the other hand, has won nothing that sticks in your memory.

It was the same for Mickelson. Fans expected great things from him when he joined the PGA Tour in 1992. One of the rare left-handers at the top levels of the game, he is tall, good-looking, wears a pleasant smile and owns one of the world's best short games.

But like Duval, Mickelson's record was missing the touch of class only winning a major event can endow. The 13 tournaments he had won earned him lots of money, but he had never played well enough to challenge in the four big events — the U.S. and British Opens, the PGA Championship and the Masters.

Mickelson made his best showing in the Open at Shinnecock Hills in 1995, but in third place after 36 holes, he closed with 72 and 74 when he needed better. He closed with 70 in the 1998 Open, but still fell eight strokes short of Lee Janzen. Mickelson had had a decent year as the Open approached, often placing high, but he hadn't won anything in more than a year.

Els, of course, had won two Opens before passing into his 30s in October 1999. He won his first at Oakmont in 1994 and his second at Congressional in 1997. He truly *won* the Congressional Open by playing a daring shot into the 17th green that saved his par as Colin Montgomerie bogeyed and Tom Lehman hooked his approach into a lake. A tough match player, he won the World Match Play Champion-

Vijay Singh was the defending PGA champion.

Payne Stewart already had one 1999 victory.

ship, at England's Wentworth Golf Club, in successive years.

But Els could be erratic. The year after he won at Oakmont, he missed the cut at Shinnecock Hills. The year after he won at Congressional, he tied for 49th place at Olympic. Still, earlier in the season, he had won at Los Angeles, where in 1995 he had thrown away the PGA Championship, and he had won the South African PGA in his homeland.

Leonard, though, seemed to be operating at a disadvantage. He had won just four tournaments since 1994, his first year as a professional. Not too impressive until you looked at them. Two were especially important. Holing every putt he looked at and sprinting through the final 18 holes in 65, Leonard made up five strokes and won the 1997 British Open. At Ponte Vedra the following spring, he played the last three rounds of The Players Championship in 69-70-67 and won by two strokes. He had won nothing since.

At 27, Leonard had the game to win anywhere. He had played consistent golf throughout the season, placed second by two strokes to Rocco Mediate at Phoenix and fourth by four strokes to Payne Stewart at Pebble Beach. He had finished among the top 10 in four of his 15 tournaments, and worse than 23rd only twice.

At the same time, he had not impressed anyone in the four Opens he had played, finishing in such remote places as ties for 68th, 50th, 36th and 40th. Yet Leonard had compiled a 1999 scoring average of 69.66, fourth best of the year, behind Duval, Woods and Davis Love III.

None of this mattered once the Open began. Forty-two-year-old Stewart had shown signs of life by winning at Pebble Beach, a tournament shortened to 54 holes by heavy rains, and 36-year-old Vijay Singh, becoming better as he grows older, had lost the Memorial to Woods by two strokes two weeks before the Open began.

BOSS

99th U.S. Open

First Round

Everyone had expected Pinehurst to play firm and fast throughout the four days of the U.S. Open, but on opening day, the Number 2 Course was soft and mildly yielding. Surprising everyone, 23 men broke par 70 and showed that this long and testing course that caused shots to bounce off-line in surprising directions and exasperating distances could be handled under these conditions. There was a reason: Rain had washed away some of its sting.

Thick overcast clouds had covered the region for days. Throughout Wednesday the humidity hovered around 95 percent, and in late afternoon, the day before the Open began, a rainstorm drenched Number 2, sending players and fans scrambling for cover. The rain slacked off for a time, but it fell heavily again in the middle of the night. The weather bureau measured an inch of rainfall over 24 hours. It softened the greens and, consequently, left them easier to hold.

While the 23 men who broke par matched the third highest in Open history, at the same time no one shot lower than 67, the highest score to lead an opening round since Payne Stewart and Woody Austin shot 67s at Oakland Hills three years earlier. Among those with 67s at Pinehurst, David Duval, who stood at the top of the world rankings, and Phil Mickelson came off the course first, about an hour and a half ahead of Billy Mayfair and, later, Paul Goydos. All four played in the morning, when Number 2 weakened.

Immediately behind them, Stewart shot 68, along with Tiger Woods, David Berganio Jr., 26-year-old Japanese professional Kaname Yokoo and unpredictable John Daly. PGA champion Vijay Singh, Brian Watts, who lost the 1998 British Open playoff to Mark O'Meara, and Justin Leonard counted among the 14 men at 69.

Pinehurst did take its toll, though. Defending champion Lee Janzen, one of two men to have won two Opens in the 1990s, stumbled in with 74, and Ernie Els, the other, shot 72. O'Meara shot 71, Davis Love III shot 70, and Tom Lehman, Fred Couples and Greg Norman shot 73. Foreign golfers didn't do well. Colin Montgomerie, who had come close to winning in 1994 and 1997, shot 72, Lee Westwood shot 73, Jose Maria Olazabal, winner of the Masters, blundered to 75, and Masashi (Jumbo) Ozaki opened with 80.

Developments of the day left little question the early starters had the advantage. Still, it was a wet, cool, uncomfortable day. The early starters played though a mist so heavy you could feel water droplets in the air and your clothes growing soggy.

Anticipating how slowly the field might play because of Number 2's severe nature, the USGA sent the first group off at 6:30, half an hour ahead of the normal time, to assure the 156-man field could finish. It was a good move; on one of the longest days of the year, the best players in the game barely finished before dark.

When Ozaki, the long-hitting Japanese golfer, struck the first shot of the round, a light fog covered Pinehurst. Neither he nor Brandel Chamblee, nor David Toms, his playing companions, could follow the flight of their drives. All three bogeyed; Number 2's first casualties.

Others followed, as the field learned how

Phil Mickelson (67) had five birdies, the most by any competitor in the first round.

David Duval (67) hit 14 greens in regulation.

David Berganio Jr. was pleased with his 68.

precisely they must gauge their shots. Playing the sixth hole, a par 3 stretched to 222 yards, both Steve Elkington and Ernie Els struck excellent shots within birdie range, slightly left of the flagstick. John Cook, the group's third member, pulled his tee shot only a trifle left of Els' ball but off line far enough to catch a slope and gallop away. Cook made 4, Els 3, and Elkington birdied, dropping to three under par.

Elkington's run didn't last. His iron from the seventh tee dived into a fairway bunker, he couldn't reach the green with his second, and he left himself an impossible shot — over a greenside bunker to a hole only 15 feet from the near edge. His pitch carried too far and ran for miles. He double-bogeyed.

Still, Carlos Franco showed that Number 2's vicious greens could be handled. An international player from Paraguay, Franco shot 69 even though he hit only six fairways and seven greens. He made up for it with amazing work around the greens. He one-putted 11 greens and chipped in for a par at the long 10th, a par 5 of 610 yards. He breezed around using only 23 putts.

Duval, on the other hand, played text-book golf, hitting fairways, hitting greens and holing a few putts. He drove especially well, hitting 10 of the 14 fairways on driving holes, and he reached 14 greens with his approach shots. Only Yokoo hit more greens than Duval with 15. A man of slight build who stands 5-foot-10 and can't weigh more than 140 pounds, Yokoo has slim arms, fragile looking wrists and wears a size medium golf glove. Nevertheless, he can smash the ball. He consistently outdrove Jerry Kelly and Bob Gilder, his pairing mates, by yards.

By hitting all those greens, Duval played a remarkably steady round. He birdied three holes and didn't make a bogey. Off at 7:30, grouped with Franco and Mickelson, he rifled a 7-iron shot to eight feet and birdied the second, then strung together 12 consecutive pars before nearly holing a 5-

Paul Goydos (67) got his only bogey at the 11th.

Billy Mayfair (67) holed three 20-foot putts.

Kaname Yokoo (67) needed 31 putts.

First Round

David Duval	67	-3
Phil Mickelson	67	-3
Billy Mayfair	67	-3
Paul Goydos	67	-3
David Berganio Jr.	68	-2
Kaname Yokoo	68	-2
Tiger Woods	68	-2
Payne Stewart	68	-2
John Daly	68	-2

iron at the 15th, a par 3. His ball rolled within two feet of the hole and he sank it. He was two under then, with three hard holes to play.

Duval made his figures at the 16th, a very difficult par 4 of 489 yards, then played a 7-iron into the 17th, still another par 3, and holed from 10 feet. A routine par 4 at

John Daly (68) birdied the first three holes.

Tiger Woods (68) birdied the last two holes.

Payne Stewart (68) was pleased with his start.

the 18th and he had his 67.

Reflecting on his round later, Duval said of his hitting so many greens, "That's how I like to play. I find it less stressful. Obviously you have to hit the ball well, and I did that today, so I very much enjoyed the day."

Strangely, neither Duval nor Mickelson had practiced much before the Open began, Duval because of his burned hand, and Mickelson because his wife, Amy, was expecting their first child at any time. Duval played only a few holes Monday to test his blistered fingers, and Mickelson didn't arrive until late Tuesday.

While Duval played extremely consistent golf, Mickelson was all over the place. Yet he matched Duval's score and actually led him most of the day. He countered Duval's birdie at the second by holing from 18 feet, and he birdied the fourth, at 566 yards the shorter of the two par 5s, and the fifth, Number 2's most dangerous hole. At 482 yards it demands a long drive and a miracle iron to a green so high above the drive zone the players can't see its contours. Mickelson struggled for those two birdies.

He missed the fourth fairway and played only a 6-iron for his second shot, but his pitching wedge braked eight feet from the hole and he holed it. The fifth was even more scary. His 5-iron approach ran about 25 feet down a slope, but he chipped in.

Three under then, his magic left him for a time. His 4-iron missed the sixth green and he chipped poorly after missing the green of the eighth, a devilish par 4 of 485 yards with steep slopes running off the sides. It was one of two holes (the 16th is the other) normally assigned a par of 5 but shortened to bring the greens within range of second shots and labeled par 4s.

Out in 34, one under par, Mickelson made no further bogeys, but he picked up two more birdies, holing a 30-footer at the

Davis Love III was not happy with his 70.

Justin Leonard (69) called his round "solid."

13th that barely caught the lip of the hole, running in another from eight feet at the 14th. Back to three under. Four solid pars and he had his 67.

Mayfair played almost as steadily as Duval, birdieing four holes and dropping a stroke at the second. He holed three 20-footers for birdies, including one at the first hole, but he three-putted the second from 25 feet. Mayfair birdied the par-5 fourth with a two-foot putt after a wedge shot from 110 yards. He birdied the par-3 ninth from 20 feet and made his final birdie at the 10th, hitting a driver, 4-iron and 8-iron to 20 feet. He parred the last eight holes.

Goydos went into the Open's first round believing every course sets up well for you if you're playing well, and he had been playing very well indeed. Actually, he had been on a streak recently; his 67 was his ninth score in the 60s in his last 15 rounds, boosting his confidence.

Whatever the reason, Number 2 had certainly suited him this day. Off to a nervous start, holing putts from eight feet and 15 feet to save pars at the first two holes, he birdied the third and reached the turn in 34, but he fell back to even par when he bunkered his approach to the 11th, his only bogey of the day.

Staging a strong finish, Goydos birdied three of the next seven and saved two other pars with deft chipping and putting.

Relaxing later, he flashed a satisfied smile and said, "I was pretty good from eight to 12 feet."

At the same time, both Woods and Daly might have caught the four leaders. Woods missed three holeable putts, a six-footer that cost him a bogey at the fifth, another from 10 feet for another bogey at the seventh and a shortish birdie putt at the 10th that he seemed to charge.

It is never wise to count this young man

Hank Kuehne (72) was co-leader of the amateurs.

Lee Janzen (74) had trouble with his approaches.

out, though. Even par after 16 holes, he played a stunning 7-iron to six feet and birdied the 17th, and a pitching wedge to 12 feet and birdied the 18th.

Daly looked as if he had a 67 safely in hand when he strode onto the 18th tee even par, but he hit the wildest kind of drive. It squirted off to the right, where it hit one of Pinehurst's towering pine trees and disappeared. While players, caddies and fans all strained to follow the ball, it smacked against the tree trunk, caromed across the fairway and onto a bare patch of ground no more than 80 or 90 yards from the tee. It must have been the shortest drive of Daly's career. After being given relief from guy wires holding a television tower in place, Daly toyed with a wooden club, but put it back and played an iron safely onto the fairway and bogeyed.

By then the clouds had flown away, the sun had come out, and trouble lay ahead.

Titleist

99th U.S. Open

Second Round

When Rees Jones rebuilt Number 2, he found the greens had shrunk from their original size. Diamondhead Corporation had used riding equipment to mow the greens, but since those mowers were too big to cut the slopes without shaving them bare, the grounds crew cut only where their mowers would work. Consequently, the edges had crept farther from danger.

In restoring the course's integrity, Jones believed he had reclaimed an average of 1,500 square feet on each green, pushing the putting surface out to the run-off downslopes that are the course's compelling feature. Any ball that caught those slopes was certain to roll away because they had been shaved so close. The USGA had had them cut quite short, which was one reason for the field's high scores.

Besides, after the sun's brief appearance Thursday afternoon, Friday turned into a beautiful day. The sky above Pinehurst shone sunny, clear and bright, with only wispy clouds in the distance. Under these pleasant conditions, the course turned cranky. The wind picked up to 10 to 15 mph, the ground dried out, greens became harder and scores shot upward.

Where 23 men had shot under par in the first round, only Payne Stewart, Jeff Maggert and John Huston broke it in the second, each with 69. Close behind them, David Duval and Phil Mickelson shot 70, along with seven others.

When the day ended, Stewart, Duval and Mickelson had tied for first place at 137, three under par. Two strokes further back, Hal Sutton and Vijay Singh shot 70 as well and matched Tiger Woods and Billy Mayfair at 139. Maggert and Huston tied at 140. Mayfair might have scored better, but after overshooting the ninth green, he played a timid chip that rolled back to him and he double-bogeyed.

David Duval (137) shot 70 in an up-and-down round after two early birdies.

Meantime, some of those who had started the day close to the leaders fell back. Tied for fifth place after 18 holes, Kaname Yokoo went from 68 to 74 and dropped out of the race. Brian Watts followed his 69 with 73, Justin Leonard, Brad Fabel and Larry Mize went from 69 to 75, and both David Berganio Jr. and John Daly, tied for fifth when the day began, blundered from 68 to 77.

It had been a hard day. The field averaged 75.44 strokes per round, nearly three strokes higher than in Thursday's first round, and 27 players failed to birdie at least one hole. Balls skipped off greens into bunkers, into deep depressions and occasionally into the woods. Dejected after shooting 78 and missing the cut, Greg Norman said he hit 12 greens but held only two of them.

Once again the fifth played exceptionally hard. Set close to a ridge, the hole seemed to be perched on the edge of oblivion. As it had a day earlier, the fifth yielded only five birdies, but it claimed more bogeys than pars (73-61), along with 10 double bogeys and five scores worse than that.

At 489 yards with a par of 4, the 16th was almost as hard. Afraid of hitting a shot over the green, most of the field played their approaches with clubs that *might* get them there rather than the one that *would* get them there. They were afraid that if the ball rolled off the back, they would face a fright-

Ernie Els (148) shot 76 to miss by one stroke.

Lee Westwood (149) dropped out after his 76.

Mark O'Meara (150) stumbled to 79.

ening downhill chip that could roll off the front, leaving them lying three where they could have been in two. They cut out the middleman.

Under conditions like that, no one took Number 2 by the throat. Some of the scores were appalling. Norman, of course, with his 78, but Mark O'Meara played worse, shooting 79. Fred Couples shot 77, Fuzzy Zoeller 77, Steve Jones, the 1996 champion, 82, and Ernie Els shot 76. European star Lee Westwood also shot 76. They all missed the cut, which fell at 147.

Lee Janzen, the defending champion, chipped in from off the last green to survive.

Two others didn't. Angered by his opening 75, Jose Maria Olazabal rammed his fist against a wall Thursday night and broke a bone in his right hand. He withdrew, along with Hale Irwin, who played six holes but came off the course with a painful shoulder.

After apologizing, Irwin said he had never walked off a course during his 31 years as a player. He said he was told he might have injured his rotator cuff, the connection in the shoulder that afflicts so many baseball pitchers.

With balls scooting from one side of the greens and off the other and players chipping two or three times, the pace of play grew obscene. By mid-morning the field had backed up as early as the second hole — one group struggling with the green, another standing in the fairway and a third waiting on the tee. As the day progressed, rounds were taking five hours; later starters took longer. Groups waited 25 minutes at the fifth tee and another 20 minutes at the sixth, the first par 3. The last group played the first nine holes in three hours and 20 minutes. Beginning at 3 p.m., they finished at 8:40.

The four first-round leaders were caught in the gridlock. Duval and Mickelson, for example, had teed off at 7:30 on Thursday, but they had an 11:30 starting time on Friday. Mayfair started at 1:10, and Goydos had the worst of it, teeing off an hour after Mayfair.

Stewart, meantime, teed off early and put up the target score with his hard-fought 69. After scrambling for pars at the first three holes, he slipped under par for the day by pitching to two feet and birdieing the fourth, played a lovely 6-iron from a sand divot at the fifth for as much of a routine par as anyone could make on this troublesome hole, birdied the seventh by holing from 12 feet. But he dropped a shot when he deliberately played away from the steep slope left of the eighth green and missed it to the right, and another at the ninth when his tee shot embedded in a greenside bunker.

Out in even-par 35, Stewart played some stray shots coming in, but he managed to save his pars. Perhaps he reached his finest moment at the 16th. Here he laid up with an 8-iron from the rough, then pitched to six feet and holed the putt for par. Earlier in the round he had saved par from a bunker at the 12th, drove into a fairway

Hal Sutton (139) had 70 with two bogeys.

Billy Mayfair (139) struggled with his putting.

Payne Stewart (137) scrambled for his 69.

Second Round

Payne Stewart	68 - 69 – 137	-3
David Duval	67 - 70 – 137	-3
Phil Mickelson	67 - 70 – 137	-3
Tiger Woods	68 - 71 – 139	-1
Hal Sutton	69 - 70 – 139	-1
Vijay Singh	69 - 70 – 139	-1
Billy Mayfair	67 - 72 – 139	-1
Jeff Maggert	71 - 69 – 140	E
John Huston	71 - 69 – 140	E

bunker but still saved par at the 14th, and birdied the 15th, the par 3, with a stunning 4-iron inside 20 feet.

After signing his scorecard, Stewart took a wry look at his day.

"Well, the score was good even if how I got it wasn't the way I envisioned. But it's what I came up with."

For a time Duval looked as if he might open a gap between himself and the field. Three under when he began, Duval holed from 30 feet and birdied the second. Four under, and now Duval stood on the dreaded fifth green preparing to putt from 30 feet once again.

Just as he lined up his putt, the scoreboard near the green showed that Mayfair had birdied the first and caught him. Without showing any emotion, Duval gave his ball a firm rap. As the ball raced toward the hole, the gallery held its breath, wondering how far past it might run if it missed. But the ball ran true and fell squarely into the hole. A birdie; five under now and leading, for Stewart had finished by then.

It didn't last. At the very next hole, Duval bunkered his tee shot, flew his recovery over the green and double-bogeyed.

From then on he battled to avoid losing more strokes. Birdies at the seventh and eighth were offset by bogeys at the ninth and 11th, where he bunkered shots on both holes, and the hard 16th, where his pitch from short of the green drifted 30 feet from

Phil Mickelson (137) thought par was great.

Vijay Singh (139) shot 70 to climb to fourth.

the hole. One over for the day now, he saved his 70 with a final birdie at the 17th, where he played a 7-iron and holed from 10 feet.

Compared with Duval's up-and-down round, Mickelson's was a study in consistency. Out in 36 after hitting his tee shot into the rough near the right bunker at the sixth, he played two drivers at the 10th, pitched to six feet and holed the putt, picking up one stroke. Even par for the day and still three under for the distance, Mickelson slipped to four under by holing from 30 feet at the 12th. Quickly, though, he fell back by bunkering his approach and bogeying the 16th.

Looking back on his round, Mickelson said he started the day believing par would be an exceptional score, because the winds were stronger and the greens had firmed up.

Analyzing Number 2, Mickelson said he

John Huston (140) birdied the 17th for 69.

Tiger Woods (139) nearly holed this putt at 16.

Jeff Maggert (140) had 69 in the second round.

liked the options the course puts before the players.

"If I or another player misses a shot, we have an opportunity to hit a great recovery and get up-and-down. I think the fifth was probably the best up-and-down I had." His 6-iron approach ran over the green, but faced with a difficult chip that could either come back to him or run off the front, he played it just right, coaxed his ball to five feet and saved his par.

While Stewart, Duval and Mickelson shot par or better, Woods struggled to stay close to the leaders. Grouped with Corey Pavin, the 1995 Open champion, and Westwood, Woods began at 7:30 and shot 71. With galleries packed five- and six-deep straining for a glimpse of him, Woods seemed a little wobbly at first. He bogeyed the fourth by blading a sand shot over the green, and the sixth by missing a seven-footer that would have saved his par. Even par for 24 holes then, Woods fought back by birdieing the ninth and 10th. Back to even par for the day, he lost one further stroke by three-putting the 14th from 50 feet.

Even so, he stood just two strokes off the lead with 36 holes still to play. Plenty of time left.

Time had run out for some great golfers, though. Playing the last year of his 10-year exemption, Curtis Strange, the only man to have won consecutive Opens since Ben Hogan in 1950 and 1951, still had a chance to survive if he could play the second nine in 34. Instead, he double-bogeyed the 12th and shot 39. With 152, he missed the cut by five strokes.

Strange was grouped with Jack Nicklaus

Curtis Strange's (152) caddie was his son, Tom.

and Sutton, all three of them North and South Amateur winners. Sutton shot 70 and tied for fourth, but Strange and Nicklaus were eliminated.

His scoring made no difference to Jack's fans. Even though he had struggled through rounds of 78 and 75 and missed the cut by six strokes, rippling applause followed him wherever he went. When he teed off at the 18th, the gallery roared so loudly that players putting on the 17th green had to stand aside until the din died down. The cheering followed him up the fairway, and as he approached the green, those in the grandstand stood and hailed him. They were disappointed to see him go.

It was sad to see Jack leave, but he had played in 43 consecutive Opens and compiled an astonishing record. But by now, another generation had already taken over.

Jack Nicklaus (153) got a rousing ovation at 18.

99th U.S. Open

Third Round

Grim-faced as he stepped off Number 2 after shooting 77 in the Open's third round, John Cook announced, "Anyone who shoots par today will have played the round of the year."

He may have been right. Of the 68 men who had survived the first two grueling days, only 33 scored 75 or better, and only six shot under 73. Steve Stricker led them all. With the help of one wonderful putt and an amazing recovery from a fairway bunker, he shot 69. Just one stroke higher, Tim Herron shot 70. They were not the men you would have expected. Meantime, with 72s, Payne Stewart, Tiger Woods, Scott Verplank and Miguel Angel Jimenez shot the next-best scores. With so many more players scoring over 75 than under, the field averaged 75.97 strokes.

Scoring had climbed so high that Stewart could lose two strokes to par and still advance into the lead. He finished the day with 209, one under par and was the only man under par for three rounds. Mickelson shot 73 and, at 210, kept within a stroke of first place. Herron and Woods tied for third at 211, and Stricker, Vijay Singh and David Duval followed with 212. Billy Mayfair was alone at 213.

To illustrate Number 2's bite, consider Duval. Tied with Stewart and Mickelson when he teed off, he shot 75, yet he lost only three strokes to Stewart and two to Mickelson. Had he shot such a high score most weeks, he would have written off that tournament and begun planning for the next. Not in this Open, though.

By shooting his 72, Woods passed Duval and climbed from a tie for fourth place to a tie with Herron for third, and with his astonishing 69, Stricker jumped 15 places, from a tie for 20th to a share of fifth place with Duval and Vijay Singh. Singh stood among the few with 73.

Except for some shift in their positions, nearly all the 13 men at the top through the first 36 holes held their ground. At the same time, Stricker, Verplank and Jimenez climbed significantly. Jimenez moved from 20th to a tie for 10th, and Verplank jumped 24 spots, from a tie for 38th to a tie for 14th.

Mayfair, Jeff Maggert and Paul Goydos stuck within reach by shooting 74s, and neither John Huston nor Hal Sutton lost much ground by shooting, in order, 75 and 76.

Others, though, bungled their way out of it. A week after winning at Memphis, Ted Tryba shot 82, and still reeling from his 77 in the second round, John Daly shot 81. Tom Kite shot 80. Bob Tway, a former PGA champion, shot 79, and Larry Mize shot 84.

Then there was Hank Kuehne, the 1998 U.S. Amateur champion. In playing the first nine in 45, his scorecard showed a 3, a 4, a 5, a 6, a 7 and an 8. If this had been poker he'd have been winning. But it wasn't; back in 36, he shot 81.

Some who survived the day were in shock. After three-putting six greens and shooting 76, Lee Janzen said he had been asked many times to name the hardest golf course he'd played. "I've got an answer now: It's Pinehurst Number 2."

Cook added, "You could bogey every hole. Pars felt like birdies."

After shooting 74, Brandel Chamblee, a rodeo fan, said, "I think being trampled by

Payne Stewart (209) took the lead despite shooting two over par.

Steve Stricker (212) had 69, the day's best score.

Tim Herron (211) eyed a birdie at the sixth.

a steer would be more fun than this."

Perhaps crossing his fingers, Verplank, on the other hand, claimed he enjoyed his day. "This was a great U.S. Open Saturday," he said. "It's the way it's supposed to be."

Stricker, of course, was beaming, especially after playing the third, one of two holes that sparked his rise. Six strokes behind the leaders after the first two days, he began the third round with a routine par at the first and followed with a 40-foot putt that fell into the hole at the second. One under for the day.

The putt had been a well-played shot; the next shot boggled the mind. Bunkered off the tee of the third, Stricker flipped an 8-iron from the sand that flew to the green, bounced once, took the backspin, jumped right and tumbled into the hole. An eagle 2. He had played two par-4 holes in five strokes. Out in 34 after losing a stroke at

Vijay Singh (212) showed his dismay after this bunker shot at the 16th, where he made a bogey.

The pairing of Tiger Woods and Phil Mickelson was eagerly followed by the large Pinehurst galleries.

Woods (211) saved par from a bunker at the 17th, shot 72 and finished two strokes behind.

Jeff Maggert (214), despite 74, was in the top 10.

the eighth, he stood three under par after 15 holes, but he bogeyed both the 16th and 17th, yet played the round of the day.

No one else found much to like about Saturday. Number 2 had grown more difficult each day, and after Friday's bright sunshine, the weather had turned sour. The mist returned, blocking out the sun, the wind picked up, and balls ran helter-skelter off greens, into bunkers and among the trees. Playing the difficult eighth, Tryba hit what looked like a perfect approach, but his ball kicked dead right off a bank and rolled to the base of a grandstand. His caddie looked at him, shook his head, then burst out laughing.

Emphasizing the troubles, Woods said, "I hit a lot of greens today. The ball didn't stay on, but I hit them."

Driving was no easier. Because of the generous width of Number 2's fairways, the players used their drivers more than usual at an Open, but on this day they had to adjust their target lines to accommodate the

Third Round

Payne Stewart	68 - 69 - 72 – 209	-1
Phil Mickelson	67 - 70 - 73 – 210	E
Tim Herron	69 - 72 - 70 – 211	+1
Tiger Woods	68 - 71 - 72 – 211	+1
Steve Stricker	70 - 73 - 69 – 212	+2
Vijay Singh	69 - 70 - 73 – 212	+2
David Duval	67 - 70 - 75 – 212	+2
Billy Mayfair	67 - 72 - 74 – 213	+3
Jeff Maggert	71 - 69 - 74 – 214	+4

wind's drift, not always easy.

Furthermore, the championship was reaching the point where, with the holes running out, every lost stroke became more difficult to make up. Some men wilted under the tension, others lived for it.

In the heat of the race, Woods said, "I love the pressure. I love playing in the most intense pressure. How can you not? This is what we play for. This is why we play hard, why we practice: to get into this position where you have to be so committed to a shot."

As he had the previous day, Woods started badly, but where he had saved himself by scraping out pars at the first two holes on Friday, he lost three strokes on Saturday. From an awkward stance beside the first green, with one foot on grass and the other in a greenside bunker, he bladed his recovery into the rough on the other side, played a bad shot trying to run the ball on with his 3-wood, chipped to 10 feet with his fourth and two-putted. After another good drive at the second, he played a 9-iron that was coming down a yard or so right of the hole, but it hit that hard green, rolled off, and now his ball lay 60 feet from the hole. Another poor shot with his 3-wood, and he bogeyed.

Woods doesn't always control his emotions, but he realized then he must concentrate on the job at hand and set about righting his listing ship. He succeeded,

Billy Mayfair (213) fell four strokes behind.

Colin Montgomerie (218) was not a contender.

Miguel Angel Jimenez (215) was tied for 10th.

playing the remaining 16 holes in one under par. It had been a wild ride, but he had played a strong round on a difficult day.

Mickelson had troubles of his own. "I hit the ball awfully sloppy. I drove poorly and hit poor irons. I just got it up-and-down quite a bit."

Indeed he did. One of the game's best scramblers, he hit only eight fairways and eight greens, and yet he scraped out a 73.

Still, it was a little disappointing. With both Stewart and Duval losing strokes, Mickelson had gone out in par 35 and led the Open by three strokes. A par 5 at the 10th and he still led, but he bogeyed the 11th, and after running off three consecutive pars, bogeyed the 15th, 16th and 17th. Then, playing one of the few good iron shots of his day, he pitched to six feet and birdied the 18th.

Optimistic, Mickelson said he felt this

Opposite, Mickelson (210) shot 73, aided by birdies at the eighth and 18th.

Darren Clarke (217) fell on the second nine.

David Duval (212) made par on the 18th for 75 after going five over par on the first eight holes.

could be his bad round of the week, saying, "If I can make this my worst round and improve on it tomorrow, I could be in good shape."

Duval sounded equally positive. Despite double-bogeying the demonic fifth and slipping five over par for the day through eight holes, he steadied himself and parred the remaining 11.

Even though he had shot 40 on the first nine and fallen three strokes off the lead, Duval insisted, "Nothing bad happened to me today." Then, showing a touch of sadism, he added, "I hope it's worse tomorrow. The harder it is, the better off I am."

In truth, Duval had reason to feel good. Although he had played some shoddy golf, he had hit 36 of the 54 greens, more than anyone else. Hitting the greens so consistently, he was still dangerous.

Stewart had a rough run as well. Even par for the day through the seventh, he bogeyed three straight holes and dropped behind Mickelson. A veteran of these battles by now, Stewart fought back and probably saved his round with a 10-foot putt for par at the 11th. It was quite a turning point, because for a time he looked as if he would bogey a fourth straight hole.

His 8-iron approach carried the green and settled in a bunker. From there he pitched out and holed the putt.

"That was a major, major factor in my round," Stewart emphasized.

From then on he played nearly flawless golf. He hit every green except the 15th, and closed his round with a 7-iron to 15 feet at the 18th and holed the putt for a closing birdie, moving ahead of the field. Once again Stewart would enter the last round in position to win the Open.

Opposite, Duval and Stewart shook hands after a round which separated them by three strokes.

99TH US

99th U.S. Open

Fourth Round

Lee Janzen had been Payne Stewart's U.S. Open nemesis. Twice in six years, Janzen had frustrated him, first at Baltusrol in 1993 and again at Olympic in 1998. Tied with five holes to play at Baltusrol, Janzen threw two birdies at Stewart, holing a memorable chip shot at the 16th, and pulled away, leaving Stewart two strokes behind.

Five years later, Stewart had taken a four-stroke lead into the last round, shot a loose 74 and lost another Open to Janzen.

Consequently, since Janzen had played three rounds of poor golf at Pinehurst, he lingered in 54th place. Forget him.

Easily done, but Stewart still could be excused for shallow breathing. Phil Mickelson, David Duval and Tiger Woods, some of the brightest young golfers of the decade, were snapping at his Achilles tendon, along with Vijay Singh, a master of style, Jeff Maggert, who had placed among the leading 10 finishers in four of the previous five Opens, Tim Herron, Steve Stricker and Billy Mayfair.

As the day played out, only Mickelson, Singh and Woods mattered. Starting three strokes back, Duval birdied two of the first three holes to close within one stroke, but quickly lost ground. Herron held on through five holes, but lost four strokes at the next three and disappeared. Mayfair had to make up four strokes but could get nothing going, and Maggert needed five strokes but lost any hope by playing the first seven holes in one over par.

In the end, Stewart fought off every one of them. Showing unsuspected strength of will, he played the shots he had to play, and at the last three holes, he holed the putts he had to hole — from 25 feet, from three feet and from 15 feet.

Payne Stewart (279) fought off his challengers with three consecutive one-putt greens.

Stewart shot 70, even par over a merciless course that broke the spirits of so many others. Considering Number 2's ruthless demands, his 72-hole score of 279 must rank among the finest four rounds of golf played in recent Opens. Even so, Stewart won by only one stroke over Mickelson, who closed with 70 and 280, even par. With 69, Singh climbed into a tie for third with Woods, who shot 70, at 281.

Stewart played such sound golf in the last round that only two men gained any ground — Singh, who might have caught him had a few more putts fallen, and Dudley Hart, who began the day in a tie for 46th place, matched Singh's 69 and improved to a tie for 17th.

It was so closely fought that except for minute errors, any of the leading four could have won. So many putts grazed the edges of holes, or disappeared inside a hole for an instant and popped out. Singh missed two in succession at the 13th and 14th. The putt at the 14th caught the lip, dipped down, but spun out. Mickelson was around the hole all day, but didn't get the birdies he might have. Woods lipped out at the 10th, three-putted from nowhere at the 11th, and missed from eight feet or so at the 17th.

The day was filled with great shots as well. Stewart nearly holed out from a bunker beside the fourth green. Woods played a marvelous approach to 12 feet at the dangerous 16th and birdied. And with the weight of the Open on his back, Stewart played a marvelous shot to three feet at the 17th. Mickelson drove in the fairway all day long, and with the Open at stake, played

Tim Herron (286) stumbled after the fifth hole.

Fourth Round

Payne Stewart	68 - 69 - 72 - 70 – 279	-1
Phil Mickelson	67 - 70 - 73 - 70 – 280	E
Vijay Singh	69 - 70 - 73 - 69 – 281	+1
Tiger Woods	68 - 71 - 72 - 70 – 281	+1
Steve Stricker	70 - 73 - 69 - 73 – 285	+5
Tim Herron	69 - 72 - 70 - 75 – 286	+6
Hal Sutton	69 - 70 - 76 - 72 – 287	+7
Jeff Maggert	71 - 69 - 74 - 73 – 287	+7
David Duval	67 - 70 - 75 - 75 – 287	+7

two fine shots into the 18th and nearly holed the putt, which could have shocked Stewart badly.

Perhaps the greatest shot of them all, certainly the most decisive, fell at the 18th green where Stewart holed a 15-foot putt not only to save par, but to save the championship. It was the last shot of the Open, and it climaxed one of the hardest fought championships in recent memory. Every one of the four men could have won, but only Stewart did. It was his second Open victory, but while he had to beat Scott Simpson in a playoff at Hazeltine National in 1991, the finish there didn't approach the tension of the last day at Pinehurst.

Once again a cool mist lay over Pinehurst, sometimes turning into rain. Clothing absorbed the dampness and grew sodden, shots splashed moisture from both the rough and the fairways, soggy pants legs dripped, and caddies spent a lot of time wiping grips. Umbrellas came out occasionally. Stewart found a novel method of staying dry; he wore a rain jacket with the sleeves cut off.

The uncomfortable conditions had no effect on Duval through the early holes. Playing with Mayfair in the fourth-from-last pairing, he saved a par from the woods at the first, then birdied the next two holes.

This was the kind of golf everyone expected from him. He had won four tournaments on the PGA Tour, including the 1999

It was a cool, misty afternoon at Pinehurst as the final competitors began play in the fourth round.

Hal Sutton (287) shot 72 to tie for seventh.

Jeff Maggert (287) could not challenge.

Steve Stricker (285) found plenty of trouble while shooting 73 in the fourth round.

Players Championship, and while he had struggled in the first five Opens he had played, he had tied for seventh in 1998. He had also climbed to the top of the world rankings.

His third round had been dismal, but now he looked as if he was about to strike. When he holed from 20 feet at the third, he had moved to even par, tying Mickelson and Woods, one stroke behind Stewart. He went no further. Two under for the day after five, he played the remaining 15 holes in seven over. Three under par after the first 36 holes, he had played the last 36 in 10 over with two 75s.

Meantime, starting 20 minutes behind Duval, Woods opened with a birdie after a super iron to four feet. Now he had joined Mickelson at even par. He didn't last either; he overshot the third green and fell back to one over.

Stewart began by pitching to 10 feet and birdieing the first, opening his lead to two strokes, bogeying the second and birdieing the third. Mickelson, meanwhile, was missing greens but saving himself with his nonpareil short game.

Throughout the first nine holes all four men played practically shot for shot. Woods lost the stroke he had won at the first, but the other three held their places, neither man gaining and only Woods losing a stroke. Stewart, Mickelson and Singh went out in 34, one under par, and Woods shot 35. Mickelson stood one stroke behind Stewart then, Singh and Woods three behind. No one else was close. Stricker and Herron had backed off, and Duval couldn't make another birdie.

The further they went, the more a playoff appeared likely. When Stewart bogeyed the 10th with a timid pitch, he dropped into a tie with Mickelson at one under par. After

Opposite, Stewart's day was no stroll in the mists as he battled to shoot even-par 70.

David Duval (287) birdied the second and third.

Tiger Woods (281) bogeyed here at the third.

Phil Mickelson (280) birdied at the seventh.

a lovely approach inside six feet, Singh had already birdied the 10th and moved to even par (he had birdied the eighth as well). Woods, though, had lipped out a birdie putt at the 10th, played a nice shot to about 15 feet at the 11th, but looking at a birdie, he three-putted. He went three strokes behind Mickelson and Stewart.

When Stewart bogeyed the 12th, Mickelson passed him. Mickelson had claimed the lead by playing a wonderfully steady round, once he had recovered from a shaky first nine, where he hit only four greens. He was driving superbly and putting well, although several putts that scorched the edges of the holes hadn't fallen.

Now they had reached the final three holes — the 16th, a par 4 of 489 yards, the longest par 4 an Open had ever seen, a 191-yard par 3 and an uphill 446-yard par 4.

The 16th: Stewart missed the green, bouncing his 2-iron second off the grassy top of a bunker, and pitched his third shot 25 feet past the hole. Seeing Stewart's shot

Stewart had to scramble to save par here at the ninth, going out in 34, one under par.

run almost off the green, Mickelson believed he had won the Open. He had missed the green as well, but he had the short game that could save him.

Here we learned never to count Stewart out. He looked different as he studied the line. His expression turned grim, his gum chewing slowed down, and you could sense his deep concentration. Once set, he stroked the ball into the hole; Mickelson bogeyed, and now Stewart had caught up.

The 17th: Two holes to go, and the tension was rising. Singh had bogeyed the 16th and stood at one over par through 17. Woods had birdied the 14th and the 16th and stood at even par, tied with Stewart and Mickelson. Now he made a mistake at the 17th. He bunkered his tee shot, pitched nicely to about eight feet, but then missed another putt. One over par again.

Now we had four men within one stroke of one another, Singh and Woods with one hole to play, Stewart and Mickelson with two. Stepping grim-faced to the tee, Stewart

Vijay Singh (281) missed this birdie try at 14.

Woods' last hope was a 35-foot birdie try on the 18th, uphill and breaking two feet to the right.

Singh also made par on the closing hole.

played a gorgeous shot three feet from the hole, and Mickelson played a shot almost as good. Stewart holed, Mickelson missed; Stewart ahead by one over Mickelson, by two over Singh and Woods.

The 18th: Both Singh and Woods parred and finished at 281. Only Stewart and Mickelson left now. His timing evidently off, Stewart pushed his drive into the deep and sodden rough. With no hope of reaching the green, he chopped out about 75 yards short of the green and pitched 15 feet short of the hole.

Mickelson, meantime, had hit another green, his 11th of the round, and got down in two putts for his par and 280.

Now Stewart was in trouble. He had left himself too long a putt to count on holing; if he missed, there would be a playoff the next day. With that off-line drive, he might have thrown away another Open.

After a long and thoughtful survey of the line, Stewart stroked the putt. His ex-

When Mickelson secured a par on the 18th, a playoff seemed likely.

pression never changing, he seemed to will the ball to fall. When it closed within two feet of the hole, he tensed. When it dropped, he whooped, raised his clenched fist, broke into the widest grin he had shown all week, and threw his arms around his caddie.

His putt may have been the longest ever holed to win an Open. There have been longer; Bobby Jones holed from 40 feet in 1930, but he beat Macdonald Smith by two strokes, and Smith finished after Jones. As far as anyone knows, no one had come to the final hole needing to hole a sizable putt to win, and holed it.

Stewart had won the Open at the age of 42, fighting off Mickelson, 29, Woods, 23, and Singh, a mature 36. Both Singh and Woods had already won tournaments of international importance, and for a time Mickelson looked as if he might join them, but like so many great players had done in the past, Stewart was just not going to let that happen.

Stewart then holed the winning 15-foot putt.

PAYNE STEWART

99th U.S. Open

The Champion

The 1990s have been like no other period since the birth of the U.S. Open golf championship. When he shot 279 at Pinehurst and fought off Phil Mickelson, Vijay Singh and Tiger Woods, Stewart became the third man to have won the Open twice in the decade. During the 1990s, Lee Janzen, Ernie Els and now Stewart have won two Opens. In no other decade had more than one man won more than one Open.

While both Janzen and Els had won their two championships before Stewart (strangely enough, they won their second Opens in successive years), there is little question Stewart had the better Open record. More specifically, he had a better record through that period than anyone.

From 1984, when he played his first Open, he has won twice, placed second twice, fifth once, sixth once, and 10th and 13th. No one else was close.

Fans first noticed Stewart in 1985, when he was beaten by two strokes and tied for fifth at Oakland Hills, and the following year at Shinnecock Hills, where he tied for sixth, beaten by four strokes.

While he hadn't much chance of winning at Oakland Hills, sitting eight strokes behind T.C. Chen, the leader, with 18 holes to play, he could have won at Shinnecock, but he might have been too inexperienced. He was 29 and playing in only his third Open. Exposed to this degree of tension for just the second time, he stumbled at the late holes, and Raymond Floyd shot 66 and won.

Nevertheless, Stewart continued to play well in the Open. He led or shared the lead after every round at Hazeltine in 1991 and won by beating Scott Simpson in a playoff. His winning was remarkable; earlier in the year he had been afraid he might never play competitive golf again. He took six weeks off because of back pains caused by a herniated disk, and wore a neck brace. It seemed to do the trick. Not only did he win the Open, he almost won again two years later. Instead, he finished second to Janzen in 1993, then did it again in 1998.

Payne Stewart became the 19th man to win the Open twice or more.

Stewart had thought of that day quite often, and he used it to inspire himself at Pinehurst.

"I learned a lot from last year. When I got home, everybody said, 'Oh, what a great try.' Well, I didn't want to hear that today. I didn't want my friends to say, 'Boy, you sure tried. It was a great effort, you're a great competitor, but bad luck.'

"I didn't want to hear that, and that motivated me."

Why some golfers play well in particular tournaments has always been a mystery. Stewart, though, believes he knows why the Open brings out the best in him.

Clutching the big trophy, Stewart proclaimed, "I love this tournament. I enjoy playing where par gets its rewards; no matter how you make them, they get their rewards. That's just my mindset at this tournament. My adrenaline is flowing more, and my concentration is better."

Because of a disappointing period of four years without winning a tournament of any kind, Stewart had not figured among the popular choices; the emphasis had shifted to younger men. Phil Mickelson, Tiger Woods and David Duval had won 29 PGA Tour events among them since 1995, and

Stewart hadn't won anything since the 1995 Houston Open.

His apparent slide didn't seem to bother him at Pinehurst, though. He played calmly and with confidence, knowing that any hole he parred would pick up a stroke on somebody.

Besides, he had prepared himself.

When he missed the cut at Memphis the previous Friday, he treated his elimination as a blessing. Now he would have a few days to study Pinehurst, determine the shots he would need, and decide how to play them. He knew Number 2 demanded an extraordinary short game, so bringing his coach, Chuck Cook, with him, he came to Pinehurst five days before the Open's first round.

"I came in here Saturday, when nobody was around," Stewart explained, "and I got a lot of good work done. I took an 8-iron, a 9-iron and a pitching wedge, and Chuck and I walked around the course. I hit a bunch of chip shots, and I hit a bunch of shots from all sorts of areas. I did it again on Sunday.

"I think my preparation was the reason I was so excited. I felt like I was very prepared for this week. I developed a game plan during my practice rounds, and I stuck to it." As an example, he never hit a driver off the first tee; instead, he played his 3-wood, and put the ball in the fairway every day.

Speaking to a packed room at the post-tournament interview, Stewart said of the last three holes, "All I wanted to do was give myself a chance."

He had just bogeyed the 15th, which let Mickelson slip past him, and then, with Mickelson feeling he'd probably win now, Stewart played a loose shot that missed the 16th green. He was in deep trouble, but he kept his resolve.

"I wasn't going to hand him the trophy," he said.

"Somehow I felt I had to chip that ball in on 16. I shouldn't have thought that way. I hit a very poor chip. When it ran 25 feet past the hole, I said to myself, 'You didn't have to do that.' "

He didn't dwell on it, though. Taking his stance and remembering his wife had told him he had been moving his head when he putted, Stewart decided on his line, went through his routine, and rapped his putt.

"I looked up, and it's going into the hole," he went on, "and off I went."

"After I make that putt, Phil makes one of his only bogeys. How many did he make today?" he asked the crowd. "He didn't make many, did he? That was it, wasn't it?" That was indeed Mickelson's only bogey.

Then the 17th. Stewart had had a particularly good ball-striking week on this hole; all four tee shots flew right at the flagstick.

"And then my putt was inside the left edge of the cup, and I made another one.

"Then I collected myself on the 18th and hit my drive. I actually thought that drive was on the fairway, but when I got up there I saw I had no chance. I couldn't even think about the green. So I took my medicine and put the ball out there where I at least gave myself a chance.

"That's what I'd done all week. When I was in a bad position I didn't compound the error by making two mistakes in a row."

Then he played the pitch that set up his last stroke of the Open.

As he studied the line, focusing all his energies on those final 15 feet, he said to himself, "You've always wanted a putt to win the U.S. Open. You've got one right now." And he holed it.

After he had won at Hazeltine, he felt that as the U.S. Open champion, he had an obligation to play better and to meet what he felt were obligations he owed to others. He didn't enjoy his year. After winning at Pinehurst, he said he had no plans to behave as he had in 1991.

"I said last night that if I won again, I'm going to enjoy this one a lot more than the first."

Caddie Mike Hicks jumped into Stewart's arms as they celebrated.

TAPN.COM
STEWART

99th U.S. Open

June 17-20, 1999, Pinehurst Number 2, Pinehurst, North Carolina

Contestant	Rounds				Total	Prize
Payne Stewart	68	69	72	70	279	$625,000.00
Phil Mickelson	67	70	73	70	280	370,000.00
Vijay Singh	69	70	73	69	281	196,792.00
Tiger Woods	68	71	72	70	281	196,792.00
Steve Stricker	70	73	69	73	285	130,655.00
Tim Herron	69	72	70	75	286	116,935.00
Hal Sutton	69	70	76	72	287	96,260.00
Jeff Maggert	71	69	74	73	287	96,260.00
David Duval	67	70	75	75	287	96,260.00
Darren Clarke	73	70	74	71	288	78,863.00
Billy Mayfair	67	72	74	75	288	78,863.00
Paul Azinger	72	72	75	70	289	67,347.00
Davis Love III	70	73	74	72	289	67,347.00
Paul Goydos	67	74	74	74	289	67,347.00
Colin Montgomerie	72	72	74	72	290	58,215.00
Justin Leonard	69	75	73	73	290	58,215.00
Dudley Hart	73	73	76	69	291	46,756.00
Jim Furyk	69	73	77	72	291	46,756.00
Jay Haas	74	72	73	72	291	46,756.00
Jesper Parnevik	71	71	76	73	291	46,756.00
Scott Verplank	72	73	72	74	291	46,756.00
John Huston	71	69	75	76	291	46,756.00
Brian Watts	69	73	77	73	292	33,505.00
Nick Price	71	74	74	73	292	33,505.00
Tom Scherrer	72	72	74	74	292	33,505.00
D.A. Weibring	69	74	74	75	292	33,505.00
Miguel Angel Jimenez	73	70	72	77	292	33,505.00
David Berganio Jr.	68	77	76	72	293	26,186.00
Tom Lehman	73	74	73	73	293	26,186.00
Geoffrey Sisk	71	72	76	75	294	23,805.00
Bob Estes	70	71	77	76	294	23,805.00
Stewart Cink	72	74	78	71	295	22,449.00
Sven Struver	70	76	75	74	295	22,449.00
Gabriel Hjertstedt	75	72	79	70	296	19,084.00
Corey Pavin	74	71	78	73	296	19,084.00
Brad Fabel	69	75	78	74	296	19,084.00
Craig Parry	69	73	79	75	296	19,084.00
Steve Pate	70	75	75	76	296	19,084.00
Carlos Franco	69	77	73	77	296	19,084.00
Esteban Toledo	70	72	76	78	296	19,084.00
Rocco Mediate	69	72	76	79	296	19,084.00
Stephen Allan	71	74	77	75	297	15,068.00
Len Mattiace	72	75	75	75	297	15,068.00
Chris Perry	72	74	75	76	297	15,068.00
Gary Hallberg	74	72	75	76	297	15,068.00
Lee Janzen	74	73	76	75	298	12,060.00
David Lebeck	74	70	78	76	298	12,060.00
Robert Allenby	74	72	76	76	298	12,060.00
Jim Carter	73	70	78	77	298	12,060.00
Brandel Chamblee	73	74	74	77	298	12,060.00

Contestant	Rounds				Total	Prize
Steve Elkington	71	72	79	77	299	10,305.00
Chris Tidland	71	75	75	78	299	10,305.00
Greg Kraft	70	73	82	75	300	9,562.00
Jason Tyska	72	74	75	79	300	9,562.00
Spike McRoy	70	74	76	80	300	9,562.00
Phillip Price	71	73	75	81	300	9,562.00
Jerry Kelly	73	74	79	75	301	8,840.00
Tom Watson	75	70	77	79	301	8,840.00
Kaname Yokoo	68	74	78	81	301	8,840.00
Tom Kite	74	72	80	76	302	8,460.00
John Cook	74	73	77	78	302	8,460.00
Bob Tway	69	77	79	78	303	8,178.00
Chris Smith	69	77	77	80	303	8,178.00
Larry Mize	69	75	84	76	304	7,966.00
*Hank Kuehne	72	75	81	78	306	Medal
Bob Burns	71	76	84	77	308	7,755.00
Ted Tryba	72	75	82	79	308	7,755.00
John Daly	68	77	81	83	309	7,543.00

Andrew Magee	73	75	148
Thomas Bjorn	70	78	148
Stephen Leaney	76	72	148
Chris Zambri	73	75	148
Ben Crenshaw	74	74	148
Scott Hoch	71	77	148
Mathias Gronberg	70	78	148
Nick Faldo	74	74	148
Ernie Els	72	76	148
Bobby Wadkins	75	73	148
Steve Flesch	75	73	148
Jim McGovern	71	77	148
Michael Muehr	74	74	148
Richard Zokol	73	76	149
Lee Westwood	73	76	149
Stuart Appleby	73	76	149
Glen Day	70	79	149
Fred Funk	71	78	149
Peter Baker	75	74	149
Scott Gump	74	75	149
Dennis Zinkon	71	78	149
Jeff Sluman	74	75	149
Sam Torrance	75	74	149
Mike Weir	73	76	149
Omar Uresti	72	77	149
Steve Lowery	74	75	149
Keith Clearwater	73	76	149
Mark O'Meara	71	79	150
Mark Brooks	74	76	150
Olin Browne	73	77	150
Bob Heintz	73	77	150
Mark Slawter	72	78	150
Notah Begay III	74	76	150
Robin Freeman	73	77	150
Fred Couples	73	77	150
Shaun Micheel	73	77	150
Bob Gilder	74	77	151
Gary March	72	79	151
Jay Williamson	73	78	151
Greg Norman	73	78	151
Barry Cheesman	72	79	151
Joey Sindelar	73	78	151
Erik Ciotti	72	79	151
Garrett Willis	77	74	151
Greg Gregory	73	78	151
Jeff Street	76	75	151
Bob Friend	74	77	151
Fuzzy Zoeller	74	77	151
Bradley Hughes	71	80	151
* Bryce Molder	73	78	151
Per-Ulrik Johansson	75	77	152
Kirk Triplett	71	81	152
Patrik Sjoland	75	77	152
Alberto Ochoa	77	75	152
Curtis Strange	78	74	152
Keith Kulzer	75	77	152
Grant Masson	74	79	153
Jeff Freeman	72	81	153
Chris Riley	74	79	153
* Andrew Barnes	74	79	153
Jack Nicklaus	78	75	153
Joe Durant	74	79	153
Mark Calcavecchia	79	74	153
Doug Barron	77	77	154
Jumbo Ozaki	80	74	154
Steve Jones	72	82	154
Craig Bowden	75	80	155
Bill Glasson	77	78	155
Jeb Stuart	77	78	155
* Tom McKnight	72	83	155
* Matt Kuchar	76	79	155
E.J. Pfister	79	77	156
Ronald Philo Jr.	77	79	156
David Toms	74	82	156
Chad Campbell	74	82	156
Jeff Gallagher	77	80	157
Retief Goosen	75	82	157
Tim Loustalot	79	78	157
Mike Stone	77	80	157
John DiMarco	79	79	158
Scott Fawcett	79	79	158
Jim White	76	83	159
Mark Mielke	78	81	159
Robert Russell	77	82	159
* Matt Call	81	79	160
Ryan Welborn	82	78	160
Hale Irwin	76		WD
Jose Maria Olazabal	75		WD

Professionals not returning 72-hole scores received $1,000 each.

*Denotes amateur.

99th U.S. Open

Statistics

Hole	1	2	3	4	5	6	7	8	9	10	11	12	13	14	15	16	17	18	Total	
Par	4	4	4	5	4	3	4	4	3	5	4	4	4	4	3	4	3	4	70	
Payne Stewart																				
Round 1	4	4	(3)	5	4	3	4	4	3	(4)	4	4	4	4	(2)	4	3	[5]	68	
Round 2	4	4	4	(4)	4	3	(3)	[5]	[4]	5	4	4	4	4	(2)	4	3	4	69	
Round 3	4	[5]	(3)	5	4	3	4	[5]	[4]	[6]	4	4	4	4	3	4	3	(3)	72	
Round 4	(3)	[5]	(3)	5	4	3	4	4	3	[6]	4	[5]	(3)	4	[4]	4	(2)	4	70	279
Phil Mickelson																				
Round 1	4	(3)	4	(4)	(3)	[4]	4	[5]	3	5	4	4	(3)	(3)	3	4	3	4	67	
Round 2	4	4	4	5	4	[4]	4	4	3	(4)	4	(3)	4	4	3	[5]	3	4	70	
Round 3	4	4	4	[6]	4	3	4	(3)	3	5	[5]	4	4	4	[4]	[5]	[4]	(3)	73	
Round 4	4	4	4	5	4	3	(3)	4	3	5	4	4	4	4	3	[5]	3	4	70	280
Vijay Singh																				
Round 1	(3)	(3)	[5]	5	4	3	[5]	4	3	5	4	(3)	4	4	3	4	3	4	69	
Round 2	4	4	4	(4)	[5]	3	4	4	(2)	5	4	4	4	4	[4]	4	3	4	70	
Round 3	[5]	4	4	(4)	4	3	4	4	[4]	5	4	4	(3)	4	[4]	[5]	[4]	4	73	
Round 4	4	4	4	5	4	3	4	(3)	3	(4)	4	4	4	4	3	[5]	3	4	69	281
Tiger Woods																				
Round 1	4	4	4	(4)	[5]	3	[5]	4	3	5	(3)	4	4	4	3	4	(2)	(3)	68	
Round 2	4	4	4	[6]	4	[4]	4	4	(2)	(4)	4	4	4	[5]	3	4	3	4	71	
Round 3	[6]	[5]	4	(4)	4	3	4	4	3	5	4	4	4	[5]	(2)	4	3	4	72	
Round 4	(3)	4	[5]	(4)	[5]	3	4	4	3	5	[5]	4	4	(3)	3	(3)	[4]	4	70	281

( ) Circled numbers represent birdies or eagles. [ ] Squared numbers represent bogeys or worse.

Hole	Yards	Par	Eagles	Birdies	Pars	Bogeys	Higher	Average
1	404	4	0	40	264	127	15	4.269
2	447	4	0	31	245	152	18	4.354
3	335	4	2	62	303	72	7	4.045
4	566	5	0	103	281	55	7	4.926
5	482	4	0	15	209	191	31	4.549
6	222	3	0	17	252	162	15	3.395
7	398	4	0	45	283	107	11	4.191
8	485	4	0	21	239	147	39	4.500
9	179	3	0	35	281	110	20	3.260
OUT	3,518	35	2	369	2,357	1,123	163	37.489
10	610	5	0	52	307	81	6	5.092
11	453	4	0	53	275	108	10	4.179
12	447	4	0	21	250	156	19	4.395
13	383	4	1	64	287	75	19	4.108
14	436	4	0	52	277	99	18	4.204
15	202	3	0	32	276	132	6	3.251
16	489	4	0	11	219	196	20	4.504
17	191	3	0	46	299	97	4	3.132
18	446	4	0	28	314	94	10	4.193
IN	3,657	35	1	359	2,504	1,038	112	37.058
TOTAL	7,175	70	3	728	4,861	2,161	275	74.547

99th U.S. Open

Past Results

Date	Winner	Score	Runner-Up	Venue
1895	Horace Rawlins	173 - 36 holes	Willie Dunn	Newport GC, Newport, RI
1896	James Foulis	152 - 36 holes	Horace Rawlins	Shinnecock Hills GC, Southampton, NY
1897	Joe Lloyd	162 - 36 holes	Willie Anderson	Chicago GC, Wheaton, IL
1898	Fred Herd	328 - 72 holes	Alex Smith	Myopia Hunt Club, S. Hamilton, MA
1899	Willie Smith	315	George Low Val Fitzjohn W.H. Way	Baltimore CC, Baltimore, MD
1900	Harry Vardon	313	J.H. Taylor	Chicago GC, Wheaton, IL
1901	*Willie Anderson (85)	331	Alex Smith (86)	Myopia Hunt Club, S. Hamilton, MA
1902	Laurie Auchterlonie	307	Stewart Gardner	Garden City GC, Garden City, NY
1903	*Willie Anderson (82)	307	David Brown (84)	Baltusrol GC, Springfield, NJ
1904	Willie Anderson	303	Gil Nicholls	Glen View Club, Golf, IL
1905	Willie Anderson	314	Alex Smith	Myopia Hunt Club, S. Hamilton, MA
1906	Alex Smith	295	Willie Smith	Onwentsia Club, Lake Forest, IL
1907	Alex Ross	302	Gil Nicholls	Philadelphia Cricket Club, Chestnut Hill, PA
1908	*Fred McLeod (77)	322	Willie Smith (83)	Myopia Hunt Club, S. Hamilton, MA
1909	George Sargent	290	Tom McNamara	Englewood GC, Englewood, NJ
1910	*Alex Smith (71)	298	John J. McDermott (75) Macdonald Smith (77)	Philadelphia Cricket Club, Chestnut Hill, PA
1911	*John J. McDermott (80)	307	Michael J. Brady (82) George O. Simpson (85)	Chicago GC, Wheaton, IL
1912	John J. McDermott	294	Tom McNamara	CC of Buffalo, Buffalo, NY
1913	*Francis Ouimet (72)	304	Harry Vardon (77) Edward Ray (78)	The Country Club, Brookline, MA
1914	Walter Hagen	290	Charles Evans, Jr.	Midlothian CC, Blue Island, IL
1915	Jerome D. Travers	297	Tom McNamara	Baltusrol GC, Springfield, NJ
1916	Charles Evans, Jr.	286	Jock Hutchinson	Minikahda Club, Minneapolis, MN
1917-18	No Championships Played — World War I			
1919	*Walter Hagen (77)	301	Michael J. Brady (78)	Brae Burn CC, West Newton, MA
1920	Edward Ray	295	Harry Vardon Jack Burke, Sr. Leo Diegel Jock Hutchison	Inverness Club, Toledo, OH
1921	James M. Barnes	289	Walter Hagen Fred McLeod	Columbia CC, Chevy Chase, MD
1922	Gene Sarazen	288	John L. Black Robert T. Jones, Jr.	Skokie CC, Glencoe, IL
1923	*Robert T. Jones, Jr. (76)	296	Bobby Cruickshank (78)	Inwood CC, Inwood, NY
1924	Cyril Walker	297	Robert T. Jones, Jr.	Oakland Hills CC, Birmingham, MI
1925	*William MacFarlane (147)	291	Robert T. Jones, Jr. (148)	Worcester CC, Worcester, MA
1926	Robert T. Jones, Jr.	293	Joe Turnesa	Scioto CC, Columbus, OH
1927	*Tommy Armour (76)	301	Harry Cooper (79)	Oakmont CC, Oakmont, PA
1928	*Johnny Farrell (143)	294	Robert T. Jones, Jr. (144)	Olympia Fields CC, Matteson, IL

Date	Winner	Score	Runner-Up	Venue
1929	*Robert T. Jones, Jr. (141)	294	Al Espinosa (164)	Winged Foot GC, Mamaroneck, NY
1930	Robert T. Jones, Jr.	287	Macdonald Smith	Interlachen CC, Hopkins, MN
1931	*Billy Burke (149-148)	292	George Von Elm (149-149)	Inverness Club, Toledo, OH
1932	Gene Sarazen	286	Phil Perkins Bobby Cruickshank	Fresh Meadows CC, Flushing, NY
1933	Johnny Goodman	287	Ralph Guldahl	North Shore CC, Glenview, IL
1934	Olin Dutra	293	Gene Sarazen	Merion Cricket Club, Ardmore, PA
1935	Sam Parks, Jr.	299	Jimmy Thomson	Oakmont CC, Oakmont, PA
1936	Tony Manero	282	Harry Cooper	Baltusrol GC, Springfield, NJ
1937	Ralph Guldahl	281	Sam Snead	Oakland Hills CC, Birmingham, MI
1938	Ralph Guldahl	284	Dick Metz	Cherry Hills CC, Englewood, CO
1939	*Byron Nelson (68-70)	284	Craig Wood (68-73) Denny Shute (76)	Philadelphia CC, West Conshohocken, PA
1940	*Lawson Little (70)	287	Gene Sarazen (73)	Canterbury GC, Cleveland, OH
1941	Craig Wood	284	Denny Shute	Colonial Club, Fort Worth, TX
1942-45	No Championships Played — World War II			
1946	*Lloyd Mangrum (72-72)	284	Vic Ghezzi (72-73) Byron Nelson (72-73)	Canterbury GC, Cleveland, OH
1947	*Lew Worsham (69)	282	Sam Snead (70)	St. Louis CC, Clayton, MO
1948	Ben Hogan	276	Jimmy Demaret	Riviera CC, Los Angeles, CA
1949	Cary Middlecoff	286	Sam Snead Clayton Heafner	Medinah CC, Medinah, IL
1950	*Ben Hogan (69)	287	Lloyd Mangrum (73) George Fazio (75)	Merion GC, Ardmore, PA
1951	Ben Hogan	287	Clayton Heafner	Oakland Hills CC, Birmingham, MI
1952	Julius Boros	281	Ed (Porky) Oliver	Northwood CC, Dallas, TX
1953	Ben Hogan	283	Sam Snead	Oakmont CC, Oakmont, PA
1954	Ed Furgol	284	Gene Littler	Baltusrol GC, Springfield, NJ
1955	*Jack Fleck (69)	287	Ben Hogan (72)	The Olympic Club, San Francisco, CA
1956	Cary Middlecoff	281	Ben Hogan Julius Boros	Oak Hill CC, Rochester, NY
1957	*Dick Mayer (72)	282	Cary Middlecoff (79)	Inverness Club, Toledo, OH
1958	Tommy Bolt	283	Gary Player	Southern Hills CC, Tulsa, OK
1959	Billy Casper	282	Bob Rosburg	Winged Foot GC, Mamaroneck, NY
1960	Arnold Palmer	280	Jack Nicklaus	Cherry Hills CC, Englewood, CO
1961	Gene Littler	281	Bob Goalby Doug Sanders	Oakland Hills CC, Birmingham, MI
1962	*Jack Nicklaus (71)	283	Arnold Palmer (74)	Oakmont CC, Oakmont, PA
1963	*Julius Boros (70)	293	Jacky Cupit (73) Arnold Palmer (76)	The Country Club, Brookline, MA
1964	Ken Venturi	278	Tommy Jacobs	Congressional CC, Bethesda, MD
1965	*Gary Player (71)	282	Kel Nagle (74)	Bellerive CC, St. Louis, MO
1966	*Billy Casper (69)	278	Arnold Palmer (73)	The Olympic Club, San Francisco, CA
1967	Jack Nicklaus	275	Arnold Palmer	Baltusrol GC, Springfield, NJ
1968	Lee Trevino	275	Jack Nicklaus	Oak Hill CC, Rochester, NY
1969	Orville Moody	281	Deane Beman Al Geiberger Bob Rosburg	Champions GC, Houston, TX
1970	Tony Jacklin	281	Dave Hill	Hazeltine National GC, Chaska, MN
1971	*Lee Trevino (68)	280	Jack Nicklaus (71)	Merion GC, Ardmore, PA
1972	Jack Nicklaus	290	Bruce Crampton	Pebble Beach GL, Pebble Beach, CA

Date	Winner	Score	Runner-Up	Venue
1973	Johnny Miller	279	John Schlee	Oakmont CC, Oakmont, PA
1974	Hale Irwin	287	Forrest Fezler	Winged Foot GC, Mamaroneck, NY
1975	*Lou Graham (71)	287	John Mahaffey (73)	Medinah CC, Medinah, IL
1976	Jerry Pate	277	Tom Weiskopf Al Geiberger	Atlanta Athletic Club, Duluth, GA
1977	Hubert Green	278	Lou Graham	Southern Hills CC, Tulsa, OK
1978	Andy North	285	Dave Stockton J.C. Snead	Cherry Hills CC, Englewood, CO
1979	Hale Irwin	284	Gary Player Jerry Pate	Inverness Club, Toledo, OH
1980	Jack Nicklaus	272	Isao Aoki	Baltusrol GC, Springfield, NJ
1981	David Graham	273	George Burns Bill Rogers	Merion GC, Ardmore, PA
1982	Tom Watson	282	Jack Nicklaus	Pebble Beach GL, Pebble Beach, CA
1983	Larry Nelson	280	Tom Watson	Oakmont CC, Oakmont, PA
1984	*Fuzzy Zoeller (67)	276	Greg Norman (75)	Winged Foot GC, Mamaroneck, NY
1985	Andy North	279	Dave Barr Chen Tze Chung Denis Watson	Oakland Hills CC, Birmingham, MI
1986	Raymond Floyd	279	Lanny Wadkins Chip Beck	Shinnecock Hills GC, Southampton, NY
1987	Scott Simpson	277	Tom Watson	The Olympic Club, San Francisco, CA
1988	*Curtis Strange (71)	278	Nick Faldo (75)	The Country Club, Brookline, MA
1989	Curtis Strange	278	Chip Beck Mark McCumber Ian Woosnam	Oak Hill CC, Rochester, NY
1990	*Hale Irwin (74+3)	280	Mike Donald (74+4)	Medinah CC, Medinah, IL
1991	*Payne Stewart (75)	282	Scott Simpson (77)	Hazeltine National GC, Chaska, MN
1992	Tom Kite	285	Jeff Sluman	Pebble Beach GL, Pebble Beach, CA
1993	Lee Janzen	272	Payne Stewart	Baltusrol GC, Springfield, NJ
1994	*Ernie Els (74+4+4)	279	Loren Roberts (74+4+5) Colin Montgomerie (78)	Oakmont CC, Oakmont, PA
1995	Corey Pavin	280	Greg Norman	Shinnecock Hills GC, Southampton, NY
1996	Steve Jones	278	Tom Lehman Davis Love III	Oakland Hills CC, Birmingham, MI
1997	Ernie Els	276	Colin Montgomerie	Congressional CC, Bethesda, MD
1998	Lee Janzen	280	Payne Stewart	The Olympic Club, San Francisco, CA
1999	Payne Stewart	279	Phil Mickelson	Pinehurst No. 2, Pinehurst, NC

*Winner in playoff; figures in parentheses indicate scores

99th U.S. Open

Championship Records

Oldest champion *(years/months/days)*
45/0/15 — Hale Irwin (1990)

Youngest champion
19/10/14 — John J. McDermott (1911)

Most victories
4 — Willie Anderson (1901, '03, '04, '05)
4 — Robert T. Jones, Jr. (1923, '26, '29, '30)
4 — Ben Hogan (1948, '50, '51, '53)
4 — Jack Nicklaus (1962, '67, '72, '80)
3 — Hale Irwin (1974, '79, '90)
2 — by 14 players: Alex Smith (1906, '10), John J. McDermott (1911, '12), Walter Hagen (1914, '19), Gene Sarazen (1922, '32), Ralph Guldahl (1937, '38), Cary Middlecoff (1949, '56), Julius Boros (1952, '63), Billy Casper (1959, '66), Lee Trevino (1968, '71), Andy North (1978, '85), Curtis Strange (1988, '89), Ernie Els (1994, '97), Lee Janzen (1993, '98), and Payne Stewart (1991, '99).

Consecutive victories
Willie Anderson (1903, '04, '05)
John J. McDermott (1911, '12)
Robert T. Jones, Jr. (1929, '30)
Ralph Guldahl (1937, '38)
Ben Hogan (1950, '51)
Curtis Strange (1988, '89)

Most times runner-up
4 — Sam Snead
4 — Robert T. Jones, Jr.
4 — Arnold Palmer
4 — Jack Nicklaus

Longest course
7,213 yards — Congressional CC, Bethesda, MD (1997)

Shortest course
Since World War II
6,528 yards — Merion GC (East Course), Ardmore, PA (1971, '81)

Most often host club of Open
7 — Baltusrol GC, Springfield, NJ (1903, '15, '36, '54, '67, '80, '93)
7 — Oakmont (PA) CC (1927, '35, '53, '62, '73, '83, '94)

Largest entry
7,889 (1999)

Smallest entry
11 (1895)

Lowest score, 72 holes
272 — Jack Nicklaus (63-71-70-68), at Baltusrol GC (Lower Course), Springfield, NJ (1980)
272 — Lee Janzen (67-67-69-69), at Baltusrol GC (Lower Course), Springfield, NJ (1993)

Lowest score, first 54 holes
203 — George Burns (69-66-68), at Merion GC (East Course), Ardmore, PA (1981)
203 — Tze-Chung Chen (65-69-69), at Oakland Hills CC (South Course), Birmingham, MI (1985)
203 — Lee Janzen (67-67-69), at Baltusrol GC (Lower Course), Springfield, NJ (1993)

Lowest score, last 54 holes
203 — Loren Roberts (69-64-70), at Oakmont CC, Oakmont, PA (1994)

Lowest score, first 36 holes
134 — Jack Nicklaus (63-71), at Baltusrol GC (Lower Course), Springfield, NJ (1980)
134 — Chen Tze-Chung (65-69), at Oakland Hills CC (South Course), Birmingham, MI (1985)
134 — Lee Janzen (67-67), at Baltusrol GC (Lower Course), Springfield, NJ (1993)

Lowest score, last 36 holes
132 — Larry Nelson (65-67), at Oakmont CC, Oakmont, PA (1983)

Lowest score, 9 holes
29 — Neal Lancaster (second nine, fourth round) at Shinnecock Hills GC, Southampton, NY (1995)
29 — Neal Lancaster (second nine, second round) at Oakland Hills CC, Birmingham, MI (1996)

Lowest score, 18 holes
63 — Johnny Miller, fourth round at Oakmont CC, Oakmont, PA (1973)
63 — Jack Nicklaus, first round at Baltusrol GC (Lower Course), Springfield, NJ (1980)
63 — Tom Weiskopf, first round at Baltusrol GC (Lower Course), Springfield, NJ (1980)

Largest winning margin
11 — Willie Smith (315), at Baltimore (MD) CC (Roland Park Course) (1899)

Highest winning score
Since World War II
293 — Julius Boros, at The Country Club, Brookline, MA (1963) (won in playoff)

Best start by champion
63 — Jack Nicklaus, at Baltusrol GC (Lower Course), Springfield, NJ (1980)

Best finish by champion
63 — Johnny Miller, at Oakmont (PA) CC (1973)

Worst start by champion
Since World War II
76 — Ben Hogan, at Oakland Hills CC (South Course), Birmingham, MI (1951)
76 — Jack Fleck, at The Olympic Club (Lake Course), San Francisco, CA (1955)

Worst finish by champion
Since World War II
75 — Cary Middlecoff, at Medinah CC (No. 3 Course), Medinah, IL (1949)

75 — Hale Irwin, at Inverness Club, Toledo, OH (1979)

Lowest score to lead field, 18 holes

63 — Jack Nicklaus and Tom Weiskopf, at Baltusrol GC (Lower Course), Springfield, NJ (1980)

Lowest score to lead field, 36 holes

134 — Jack Nicklaus (63-71), at Baltusrol GC (Lower Course), Springfield, NJ (1980)

134 — Chen Tze-Chung (65-69), at Oakland Hills CC (South Course), Birmingham, MI (1985)

134 — Lee Janzen (67-67), at Baltusrol GC (Lower Course), Springfield, NJ (1993)

Lowest score to lead field, 54 holes

203 — George Burns (69-66-68), at Merion GC (East Course), Ardmore, PA (1981)

203 — Chen Tze-Chung (65-69-69), at Oakland Hills CC (South Course), Birmingham, MI (1985)

203 — Lee Janzen (67-67-69), at Baltusrol GC (Lower Course), Springfield, NJ (1993)

Highest score to lead field, 18 holes

Since World War II

71 — Sam Snead, at Oakland Hills CC (South Course), Birmingham, MI (1951)

71 — Tommy Bolt, Julius Boros, and Dick Metz, at Southern Hills CC, Tulsa, OK (1958)

71 — Tony Jacklin, at Hazeltine National GC, Chaska, MN (1970)

71 — Orville Moody, Jack Nicklaus, Chi Chi Rodriguez, Mason Rudolph, Tom Shaw, and Kermit Zarley, at Pebble Beach (CA) Golf Links (1972)

Highest score to lead field, 36 holes

Since World War II

144 — Bobby Locke (73-71), at Oakland Hills CC (South Course), Birmingham, MI (1951)

144 — Tommy Bolt (67-77) and E. Harvie Ward (74-70), at The Olympic Club (Lake Course), San Francisco, CA (1955)

144 — Homero Blancas (74-70), Bruce Crampton (74-70), Jack Nicklaus (71-73), Cesar Seduno (72-72), Lanny Wadkins (76-68) and Kermit Zarley (71-73), at Pebble Beach (CA) Golf Links (1972)

Highest score to lead field, 54 holes

Since World War II

218 — Bobby Locke (73-71-74), at Oakland Hills CC (South Course), Birmingham, MI (1951)

218 — Jacky Cupit (70-72-76), at The Country Club, Brookline, MA (1963)

Highest 36-hole cut

155 — at The Olympic Club (Lakeside Course), San Francisco, CA (1955)

Most players to tie for lead, 18 holes

7 — at Pebble Beach (CA) Golf Links (1972); at Southern Hills CC, Tulsa, OK (1977); and at Shinnecock Hills GC, Southampton, NY (1896)

Most players to tie for lead, 36 holes

6 — at Pebble Beach (CA) Golf Links (1972)

Most players to tie for lead, 54 holes

4 — at Oakmont (PA) CC (1973)

Most sub-par rounds, championship

124 — at Medinah CC (No. 3 Course), Medinah, IL (1990)

Most sub-par 72-hole totals, championship

28 — at Medinah CC (No. 3 Course), Medinah, IL (1990)

Most sub-par scores, first round

39 — at Medinah CC (No. 3 Course), Medinah, IL (1990)

Most sub-par scores, second round

47 — at Medinah CC (No. 3 Course), Medinah, IL (1990)

Most sub-par scores, third round

24 — at Medinah CC (No. 3 Course), Medinah, IL (1990)

Most sub-par scores, fourth round

18 — at Baltusrol GC (Lower Course), Springfield, NJ (1993)

Most sub-par rounds by one player in one championship

4 — Billy Casper, at The Olympic Club (Lakeside Course), San Francisco, CA (1966)

4 — Lee Trevino, at Oak Hill CC (East Course), Rochester, NY (1968)

4 — Tony Jacklin, at Hazeltine National GC, Chaska, MN (1970)

4 — Lee Janzen, at Baltusrol GC (Lower Course), Springfield, NJ (1993)

Highest score, one hole

19 — Ray Ainsley, at the 16th (par 4) at Cherry Hills CC, Englewood, CO (1938)

Most consecutive birdies

6 — George Burns (holes 2–7), at Pebble Beach (CA) Golf Links (1972) and Andy Dillard (holes 1-6), at Pebble Beach (CA) Golf Links (1992)

Most consecutive 3s

7 — Hubert Green (holes 10–16), at Southern Hills Country Club, Tulsa, OK (1977)

7 — Peter Jacobsen (holes 1–7), at The Country Club, Brookline, MA (1988)

Most consecutive Opens

43 — Jack Nicklaus (1957-99)

Most Opens completed 72 holes

35 — Jack Nicklaus

Most consecutive Opens completed 72 holes

22 — Walter Hagen (1913-36; no Championships 1917-18)

22 — Gene Sarazen (1920-41)

22 — Gary Player (1958-79)

Robert Sommers is the former editor and publisher of the USGA's *Golf Journal*, author of *The U.S. Open: Golf's Ultimate Challenge* and *Golf Anecdotes*, and is based in Port St. Lucie, Fla.

Michael Cohen is a photographer based in New York City and a contributor to many magazines and books.

Fred Vuich is a staff photographer for *Golf Magazine*, a contributor to many books, and is based in Pittsburgh.

99th U.S. Open Championship

Pinehurst Number 2

June 17-20, 1999

Par and Yardage

Hole	Par	Yardage	Hole	Par	Yardage
1	4	404	10	5	610
2	4	447	11	4	453
3	4	335	12	4	447
4	5	566	13	4	383
5	4	482	14	4	436
6	3	222	15	3	202
7	4	398	16	4	489
8	4	485	17	3	191
9	3	179	18	4	446
	35	3,518		35	3,657
				70	7,175